Edited by SARAH WIDDICOMBE

THE
SOUND
HORSE
BIBLE

THE COMPREHENSIVE GUIDE TO MAINTAINING SOUNDNESS IN YOUR HORSE'S BACK, LEGS AND TEETH

D&C
David and Charles

your
horse

A DAVID & CHARLES BOOK

First published in the UK in 2006

Layout and design copyright © David & Charles
Source material courtesy of *Your Horse* magazine
© Emap Active

David & Charles is an F&W Publications Inc. company
4700 East Galbraith Road
Cincinnati, OH 45236

A catalogue record for this book is available from the
British Library.

ISBN-13: 978-0-7153-2240-6
ISBN-10: 0-7153-2240-0

Printed in China by SNP Leefung
for David & Charles
Brunel House   Newton Abbot   Devon

Commissioning Editor: Jane Trollope
Art Editor: Sue Cleave
Desk Editor: Jessica Deacon
Project Editor: Sarah Widdicombe
Production: Beverley Richardson
Veterinary Consultant: John Killingbeck, BSc BVM&S
   Cert EP MRCVS

Visit our website at www.davidandcharles.co.uk

David & Charles books are available from all good
bookshops; alternatively you can contact our Orderline
on 0870 9908222 or write to us at FREEPOST EX2
110, D&C Direct, Newton Abbot, TQ12 4ZZ (no stamp
required UK only); US customers call 800-289-0963 and
Canadian customers call 800-840-5220.

The publishers wish to thank the following contributors,
whose original articles for *Your Horse* magazine were
used in this book:

Sue Armstrong MA Vet MB, Vet MF Hon, MRCVS;
Stephen Ashdown MA, Msc, MRCVS Bvet Med;
Neal Ashton Bvet Med, Cert EP, MRCVS; Jane Baker
BHS SM, BHSII; Ellie Bolton BHSI SM; Julie Brown;
Jo Butler BHSAI; Chris Caden-Parker; Milla Healey; Tim
Couzens BVet Med, MRCVS, Vet MF Hon;
Caroline Dawson; Margaret Donnelly; Lizzie Drury BSc
(Hons); Dr Melinda Duer; Robert Eustace BVSc, Cert EP,
FRCVS; Eileen Gillen; Natalie Griffiths BSc (Hons), Ost Dip
Animal Ost; Pat Harris MA, PhD, Dip ECVCN, VetMB,
MRCVS; Theresa Hollands BSc (Hons), MSc (Nutrition),
R Nutr; Victoria Jackson; Chris Johannson BVM&S, Cert EP,
MRCVS; Kate Jones BSc (Hons); John Killingbeck BSc,
BVM&S, Cert EP, MRCVS; Amelia Knox; Mia Korenika BHSII,
HND; Mark Lainchbury BVSc, MRCVS; Cathy Lammie;
Claire Lilley; Philip Lindley BHSI, Cert Ed; Mark Lingard
BVSc, DVR, MRCVS; Clare Lockyer BSc (Hons), R Nutr;
Allison Lowther; Katie Lugsden BSc (Hons); Carol Mailer;
Lucy McGarity BSc (Hons), PG Dip AM; Andrea McHugh;
Elizabeth McQuillan; Clive Meers-Rainger; Helen Millbank;
Daniel Mills SVSc, MRCVS; Michael Peace; Sarah Redden;
Terri Richmond; Julian Rishworth BVet Med, MRCVS;
Alison Ritchie BHS Int, BHS stage 4 horse care instructor;
Nikki Routledge PGD, BSc (Hons), BHSAI, EBW;
Dena Schwartz FICHT; Jane Shepherd; Amanda Sutton MSc
Vet Physio, MCSP, SRP, GDP; Anna Thompson;
Justine Thompson; Tammy Thurlow; Glyn Trundle DWCF;
Sophie Underwood; Jane Vargerson BHS SM; Hilary Vernon;
Heidi Wealleans BSc (Hons); Charles Wilson MA, BHSAI;
Alison Woulds

and also Natasha Simmonds, *Your Horse* editor, and Susan
Voss and her team at Emap Licensing.

PHOTO ACKNOWLEDGMENTS
Photography by Matthew Roberts and Bob Languish.

Contents

Using this book

This book is designed as a user-friendly guide to soundness, and the common causes of unsoundness, in the horse. Focusing on the horse's teeth, back, legs and feet, the aim is to provide owners with everything they need to know in order to keep their horses sound, and to identify and deal with problems as and when they arise.

As a foundation for understanding exactly how a horse 'works', the first section of the book explains how he is constructed, what he is made of, and how the various parts of his body function, both individually and together. Since prevention is always better than cure, the next section describes in detail the steps you, the owner, can take to keep your horse healthy and sound. It provides information on a wide range of topics, from keeping up to date with dental check-ups, ensuring your horse's saddle fits correctly and training for fitness, to how to assess your horse on a daily basis and spot potential problems at an early stage.

It also explains how to make the most of the expertise offered by your farrier and vet: often your best friends when it comes to maintaining your horse's soundness. You should read these two sections before going any further.

The rest of the book deals with specific problems you may encounter with your horse and is divided into three parts: teeth, back, and legs and feet. Each section opens with advice on how to recognize when your horse is having difficulties in a particular area – not always an easy task. This is followed by descriptions of a range of soundness problems, their symptoms, diagnosis and recommended treatments, all presented in clear, non-technical language (just in case, a Glossary is provided on pages 182–183). Special features cover related topics such as bitting problems, controlling your horse's weight or coping with a horse that is on box rest – all essential areas to understand if you are to keep your horse happy, healthy and sound.

1 Functions and physiology

If you are to care for your horse properly and keep him sound, you need to understand how he is put together and how the various parts of his body fulfil their functions as nature intended.

In this section

Teeth

The horse's teeth are absolutely essential for his survival. Put simply, they are required to get food from fields, haynets or buckets into his digestive tract. Any failure in this process is usually painful for the horse and involves food wastage and quidding (spilling food from the mouth). It also contributes to ill-health and weight loss.

Teeth lie at the entry to the digestive system and provide the means of selecting, grabbing and grinding food to form it into a bolus (round mass), which can be swallowed and propelled down the oesophagus (throat) to the stomach.

The lips of the horse, especially the top lip, are very effective tools for searching out and lining up potential food for the first line of teeth – the incisors. A horse's lips are used in almost the same way that we use our hands to search around for the best potato crisp in the packet.

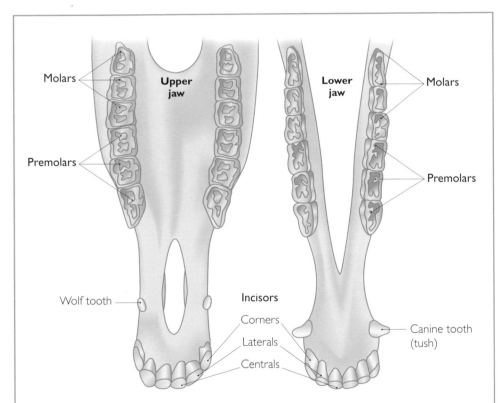

Incisors
The incisors are the 12 teeth visible when you raise the horse's upper lip. They are normally considered to be the three teeth on either side of the midline, both top and bottom. The pair in the middle are called centrals, the next pair laterals and the outer teeth are corner teeth.

Molars
There are three premolars on the top and bottom arcades of teeth on both sides, and three molars behind these, again on both sides and top and bottom. The top and bottom arcades of teeth meet at an angle, with the upper teeth coming to a cutting edge outside the lower arcade of molars and premolars. Equally, the lower teeth form a cutting edge inside the line of upper teeth.

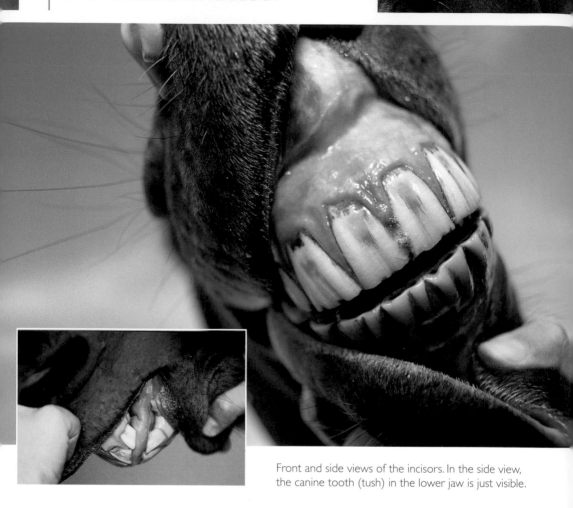

Front and side views of the incisors. In the side view, the canine tooth (tush) in the lower jaw is just visible.

Wolf and canine teeth (tushes)

There is an extra premolar in front of the upper arcade called a wolf tooth. It has little purpose and is often linked with a variety of controversial problems. Less importantly, horses have canine teeth or tushes. These have little real purpose and rarely cause a problem.

The incisors meet with flat surfaces, which are able to hold the forage in a vice-like grip – as anyone whose fingers have been mistaken for a carrot will tell you. The edges are sharp and the horse's head moves to tear the forage against these edges, chopping it away from the roots.

The resulting food mass is manipulated by the strong tongue to line it up for grinding by the premolars and molars. Both types of teeth are much more difficult to view as they line the cheeks of the horse.

The molars and premolars grind the food to break down herbivorous forage into a finely chopped, soggy mulch which, when mixed with saliva, is chewed and turned into a bolus that can be deliberately swallowed.

Wear and tear

To survive, horses must eat large volumes of herbivorous food in order to get adequate nutrition. This involves almost constant chewing. Because the food has a relatively low nutritional content, with the plant cells being surrounded by an indigestible case, considerable grinding is needed. The constant chewing by the horse inevitably wears away his teeth. To counter this, herbivores evolved with slow-growing teeth that replace themselves as they are ground down.

Teeth, chewing and digestion

Teeth are a vital part of the digestive process and the key to the success of the rest of the system – and even the mental state of the horse. There are two aspects to this.

Psychological need

Horses have a psychological need to chew – deprive them of this through diet and they will turn to alternative chewing options. Ponies in bare paddocks chew fence posts, hedges, soil or

Horses consume a huge volume of herbivorous food, which means almost constant chewing.

How much does he chew?

4,600 (no. of chews to eat 1kg) ÷ 3,600 (no. of chews in 1 hour) = 1.27 hours to eat 1kg hay

If a 500kg horse is fed ad-lib forage:
1.27 hours x 12.5kg = 16 hours

This means that 60% of the horse's time is occupied by chewing. This satisfies his psychological need to chew.

If a 500kg horse, working hard, is fed 60% forage and 40% concentrates:
8kg hay (chews 4,600 times per kg) = 36,800 chews
4kg concentrates (chews 1,200 times per kg) = 4,800 chews
Total number of chews = 41,600

Time occupied = 41,600 (total chews) ÷ 3,600 (chews in 1 hour) = 11.5 hours

This means that 48% of the horse's time is occupied by chewing. This is unlikely to satisfy his psychological need to chew.

Chewing produces saliva, which contains enzymes and antacids to buffer stomach acid.

At risk

Racehorses are most at risk of ulcers. These horses are lucky if they receive 40% fibre in their diet. They will produce 35 litres (8 gallons) less saliva a day than a horse fed ad lib, so may develop the same problems as a laminitic pony or any other horse whose diet is being restricted.

droppings. Horses stabled without adequate chewing material in their diet will opt to chew their beds, stable doors, droppings or mangers.

A horse takes roughly one chew per second, but the number of chews he makes varies according to the food you give him. If you work out how many chews your horse will make, you can tell whether or not you are feeding him enough to keep him occupied (see panel on page 9).

Your horse needs to chew – find him with an empty haynet in the morning or put him out in a bare paddock without additional hay and you are preventing him from using his teeth as he should. He is likely to find alternative ways of satisfying his psychological need to chew.

Physiological need

Horses also have a physiological need to chew – they only produce saliva when they are physically chewing. Saliva is required as a lubricant to aid swallowing and prevent the horse choking. It also passes into the acid stomach, where it acts as a buffer for the food and helps to prevent ulcers.

Horses are the only herbivores that physically chew their food before swallowing. Their teeth have only one chance to process the food mechanically, so problems with teeth and mouths affect digestion relatively quickly.

Now that the role and importance of teeth has been established, we can see how important dental care is for horses. Regular attention can help to prevent a whole host of problems.

Effects of teeth rasping

A research study looked at the effect of lack of dental care on a group of horses. Researchers monitored the intake of hay before and after rasping, the faecal particle size before and after rasping, and the number of chews the horses took.

Results showed that horses with poor dentition take more chews to eat the same weight of hay than they do after their teeth have been rasped, but they are less effective at processing the fibre as longer lengths show up in the droppings.

In addition, because they spend more chews trying to process the fibre, they are unable to eat as much hay in total.

Saliva production is also compromised because it takes longer for horses with poor dentition to eat the same weight of hay. Such horses in fact make fewer chews per minute and therefore produce less saliva.

The length of fibre in a horse's droppings gives an indication of the efficiency of his digestion and the state of his teeth.

A horse at grass will fulfil all his needs: nutritional, physiological and psychological.

Structure

Conformation is largely determined by your horse's skeleton, and understanding your horse's skeleton is a great way to see how and why he is put together the way he is. His appearance should tell you not only what it is possible for him to do, but much of what he has already done. Your horse is like a book: if you know how to read him he will tell you a story.

When you look at the points of your horse, remember that they are simply where the underlying bones can be felt at the skin's surface (see overleaf).

Bones

Bone may be stiff and hard, but it is not dead. It is living tissue, with a blood supply bringing nutrients and minerals that provide the building blocks for its continual renewal and remodelling.

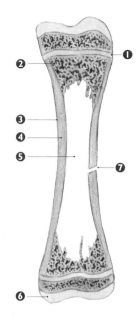

Cross-section through bone

❶ Physis (growth plate)
❷ Cancellous bone
❸ Periosteum
❹ Corticol bone
❺ Medullary cavity
❻ Articular cartilage
❼ Nutrient foramen (through which nutrient artery enters bone)

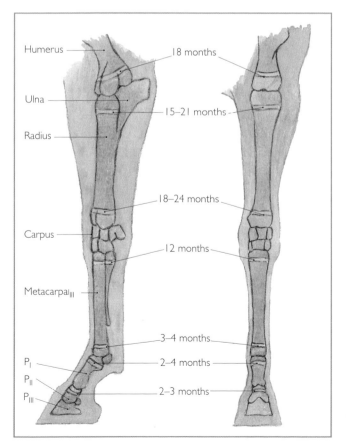

Humerus

18 months

Ulna

15–21 months

Radius

18–24 months

Carpus

12 months

Metacarpal₃

3–4 months

P₁

2–4 months

P₁₁

P₁₁₁

2–3 months

Closure times
of growth plates
(see page 17)

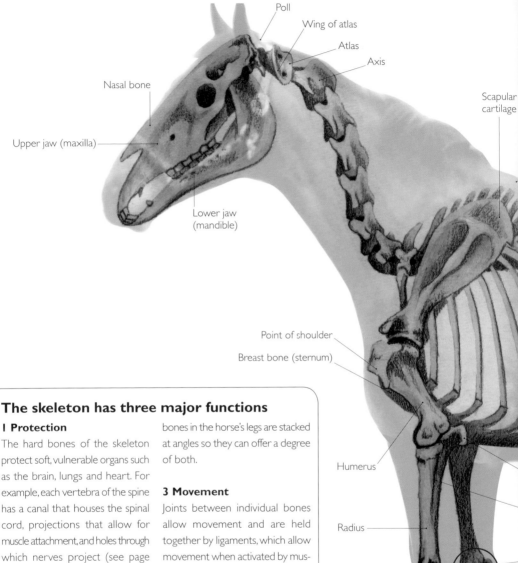

Poll

Wing of atlas

Atlas

Axis

Scapular cartilage

Nasal bone

Upper jaw (maxilla)

Lower jaw (mandible)

Point of shoulder

Breast bone (sternum)

Humerus

Radius

Splint bone (metacarpal$_{IV}$)

The skeleton has three major functions

1 Protection

The hard bones of the skeleton protect soft, vulnerable organs such as the brain, lungs and heart. For example, each vertebra of the spine has a canal that houses the spinal cord, projections that allow for muscle attachment, and holes through which nerves project (see page 19).

2 Support

The horse's heavy body and neck would be best supported by four rigid pillars, one at each corner. Stable and strong as this would be, the horse would have about as much mobility as a table. The whole skeleton is a compromise between support and movement, and the bones in the horse's legs are stacked at angles so they can offer a degree of both.

3 Movement

Joints between individual bones allow movement and are held together by ligaments, which allow movement when activated by muscles and tendons. The horse's body has been designed with most of his muscles above the knee and hock, so his legs stay light and easy to manoeuvre.

Joints occur where two or more bones meet. They may be immobile, slightly mobile or freely mobile. Freely mobile joints have a specialized structure called a synovial joint (see page 127).

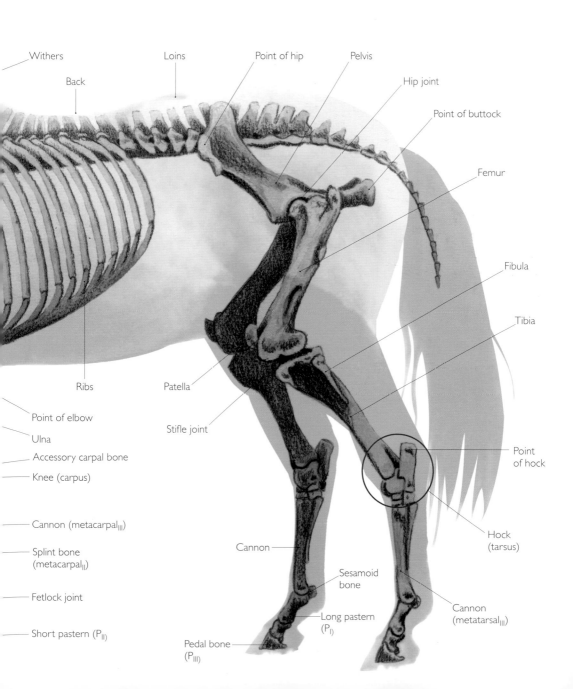

Withers

Back

Loins

Point of hip

Pelvis

Hip joint

Point of buttock

Femur

Fibula

Tibia

Ribs

Point of elbow

Ulna

Accessory carpal bone

Knee (carpus)

Cannon (metacarpal$_{III}$)

Splint bone
(metacarpal$_{II}$)

Fetlock joint

Short pastern (P$_{II}$)

Patella

Stifle joint

Cannon

Sesamoid
bone

Long pastern
(P$_{I}$)

Pedal bone
(P$_{III}$)

Point
of hock

Hock
(tarsus)

Cannon
(metatarsal$_{III}$)

In young foals, bone is still being laid down in the majority of the growth plates in their limbs and other areas of the skeleton.

It is by continually rebuilding new bone tissue that the skeleton can respond to exercise. The tissue becomes denser and it is this that helps the bone recover from traumas such as cracks or fractures. Rebuilding bone tissue also helps the bone respond better to an uneven load or repeated out-of-range movements by producing a bony lump.

In a young horse, bone growth occurs in specialized areas called growth plates, where soft cartilage is turned into hard bone by the deposition of protein and minerals. These growth plates close at different rates (see page 13). The last growth plates to close are in the spine and withers and some of these do not close until 4 years of age – this should be considered when fitting a saddle on a young horse.

Muscles

It is the layers of muscle that fill out the form of the horse. Joints allow movement, but actual movement is not possible without a muscle or series of muscles contracting around a joint to bring movement about.

Muscles work in pairs: as one works to contract and shorten, the other will relax and lengthen. They work in three main ways, contracting to:

■ stabilize a joint;

■ move a joint;

■ prevent movement of a joint.

Muscle works on a 'use it or lose it' principle. When a muscle contracts it gets shorter, rounder and tenser. Repeated contractions during a movement sequence result in the muscle concerned becoming more developed, by muscle fibre cells either getting bigger or increasing in number.

If the muscle is to develop in the right way, it must move correctly. If the muscle does not develop as it should, it is very important to consult a vet in order to work out why it is being used incorrectly, before attempts are made to 'retrain' or 'rebalance' the horse.

Tendons from the muscles above the knee facilitate movement of the bones below it – for example, allowing the forelegs to fold when jumping.

Tendons

An essential part of muscle structure is the muscle tendon. Tendons run from muscle to bone. When a muscle contracts, it pulls on its tendon and moves the bone on which the tendon is inserted. Below the knee and hock of the horse there are no muscles – movement of the component bones of the lower limb is via the long tendons running from muscles above the knee and hock (see page 27).

Tendons have a very specialized structure. The fibres of the tendon are crimped, or wrinkled, and when it is stretched (by its muscle contracting), especially when the bones and joints are weight bearing, the crimp straightens out, allowing more stretching. When the loading (or weight-bearing period) ends, the crimp is restored. This results in an elastic recoil movement (like an elastic band being released), and this property is used to move the lower limb forward as the hoof comes off the ground. Normally this action is repeated without any change except to generate some heat, which is dispersed naturally, although abnormal conditions can lead to overheating (see page 26). However, significant heat only develops in the large muscle masses.

Like bone, tendon responds to loading positively by becoming more resilient, but the process takes longer.

How does the horse carry a rider?

The horse's skull, vertebral spine, ribs and tail make up his axial skeleton. It is the sequence of these different types of bone that give him maximum stability for carrying weight.

Most of the weight your horse would naturally carry (without you on top) lies beneath the spine. Cleverly, this weight has the effect of locking the horse's spine into position so that it cannot bend in the direction of the load. Fortunately for us, this also makes it capable of supporting a rider without sagging in the middle – a fact that is purely coincidental.

Skull

The horse's skull is basically a bony box protecting the brain. These bones are quite light compared to the heavier bone of the lower jaw, which houses the teeth, because the bone is of lower density and also has airspaces – sinuses – within it.

Vertebrae

The brain continues out of the skull as the spinal cord, which is protected by the vertebrae of the neck and spine. These are bony, block-like structures that overlap and interlock with each other. Each is cushioned from the next by an intervertebral disc of cartilage (see above right).

Sticking out from each vertebra are various projections called processes. These extend upwards (the dorsal spinous processes – dorsal spine for short) and sideways (the transverse processes). They also articulate with each other. Their size and shape varies along the spine, as does the degree of movement in different sections of the column. The neck, for example, is relatively mobile, while the mid-back and loins are relatively immobile.

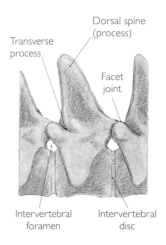

Dorsal spine (process)

Transverse process

Facet joint

Intervertebral foramen

Intervertebral disc

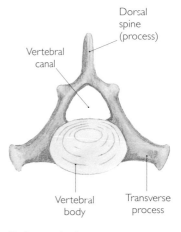

Dorsal spine (process)

Vertebral canal

Vertebral body

Transverse process

Basic vertebral structure

In between each pair of vertebrae is a pair of spinal nerves – one each side of the spine – which leave the spinal cord to travel to different areas of the body. Too much movement between the horse's vertebrae would put the integrity of these nerves at risk.

Ligaments

Although the spine has a little movement in some areas, due to muscles contracting and relaxing, this movement is contained within safe limits by bone-to-bone connective ligaments. These ligaments also constrain the movement of the individual vertebrae, so there is much less chance of the spinal cord and individual nerves being damaged.

The cervical spine – the length from behind the horse's ears to the withers – has more flexibility than any other area of the axial skeleton. This area is also stabilized by ligaments: this time a sheet of them known as the nuchal ligament. The area of least movement in the spine is the sacral ligament – the area just

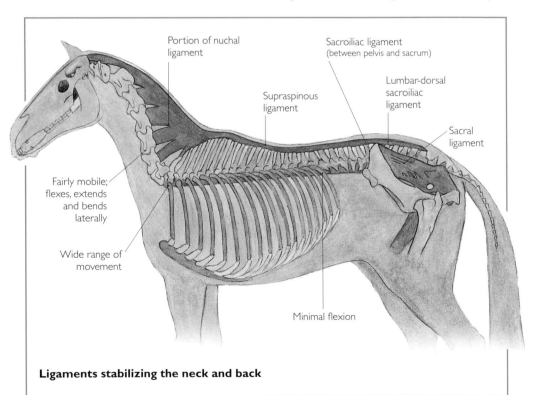

Portion of nuchal ligament

Sacroiliac ligament (between pelvis and sacrum)

Supraspinous ligament

Lumbar-dorsal sacroiliac ligament

Sacral ligament

Fairly mobile; flexes, extends and bends laterally

Wide range of movement

Minimal flexion

Ligaments stabilizing the neck and back

before the tail. The central back area, where we sit, is the thoracic spine, where some lateral and dorso-ventral movement is possible, as can be seen in a horse arching his back or bucking.

Running from the head to the sacrum is a very strong ligament named the supraspinous ligament. This attaches to the top of all the dorsal spinous processes and acts like a massive elastic band, imparting stability and some flexibility. Muscles that provide movement lie longitudinally in the spaces between the bodies and processes of the vertebrae. The spine is also stabilized by an overlapping layer of muscles wrapped around, across and along the spinal tube.

This description should demonstrate the great rigidity and strength of the horse's spine, particularly in the area of the saddle. A quadruped such as the horse, with his horizontal backbone, must have a strong vertebral column to support the massive weight of his abdominal contents and the huge forces exerted through the hindlimbs during locomotion.

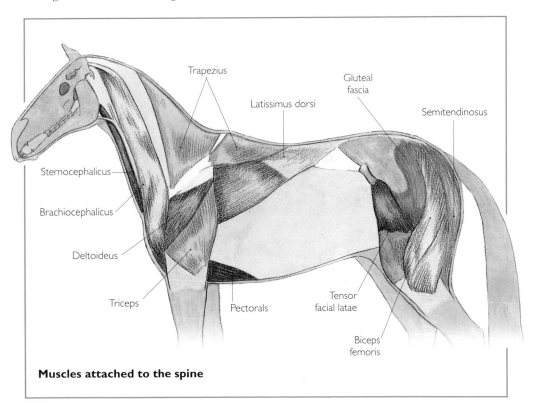

Muscles attached to the spine

Structure of the spine

❶ **Atlas/axis** A specialized joint, this allows up/down and side-to-side movement.

❷ **Cervical vertebrae (7)** These form an 's' shape, rather than following the crest of the neck. They are the largest vertebrae with broad articulations, called facet joints, which overlie each neighbouring vertebra and permit a wide range of movement in all directions.

❸ **Thoracic vertebrae (18)** These start just in front of the shoulder blade and form the major part of the back in a near-horizontal plane. They attach to, and articulate with, the head of each rib and extend back to just behind the saddle. These vertebrae are smaller and interlock tightly, permitting only minimal movement between adjacent vertebrae although some sideways movement can be made by contraction of the muscle between the ribs. The difference in shape of the processes on each vertebra is greatest among the thoracic vertebrae, the tallest dorsal processes giving rise to the withers.

❹ **Anticlinal vertebra** This sticks straight up, effectively preventing the back bending the wrong way by locking dorsal spines facing the tail against those facing the head.

❺ **Lumbar vertebrae (usually 6)** These have broad transverse processes and reduced dorsal spines, for attachment of stabilizing muscle and muscles for moving the hindlimbs. The last lumbar vertebra has a large articular surface on each transverse process which connects to the wing of the sacrum.

❻ **Lumbo-sacral junction** This allows some side-to-side and rotational movement – think of a gelding urinating or a racehorse coming out of the starting stalls.

❼ **Sacral vertebrae (5)** These are fused together into a solid triangular mass which lies under the top of the rump. There is no movement between the bones, but they provide a broad attachment surface for ligaments and muscles. The sacrum forms a junction with the pelvis at the sacroiliac joint, but this is not a true joint, in that its function is to provide a stable anchorage for the pelvis and the massive leverage of the hindlimbs.

❽ **Coccygeal vertebrae (15–21, usually around 18)** These form more or less a tube for the end of the spinal cord and gradually reduce in size to form the tail.

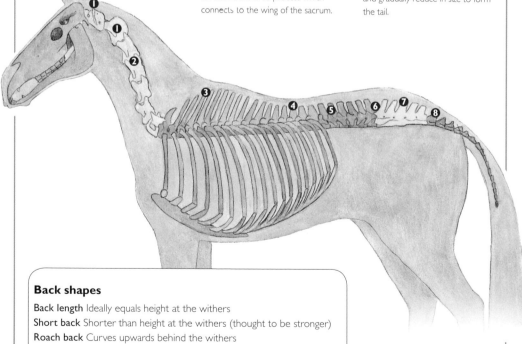

Back shapes

Back length Ideally equals height at the withers
Short back Shorter than height at the withers (thought to be stronger)
Roach back Curves upwards behind the withers
Sway back Dips down excessively
Weak loins Poor muscle
Slab-sided Ribs do not curve out enough

How the spine shapes the back

Now you know the basics about the workings of your horse's spine, you can use it to improve your riding and general management of your horse. Remember to bear his conformation in mind for saddle fitting, for instance, as it is vital not to pinch vertebrae or restrict movement (see pages 42–43).

Take your horse's saddle off and have a good look at his spine. His neck length is dictated by his need to reach down to the grass. The shape of his back will depend on the make-up of his vertebrae, and there will also be differences of back outline depending on breed and parentage.

Withers

The bump in outline at the base of the horse's neck is the withers. The muscles in this area will support the saddle, together

with the ribs, so their shape is very important, especially when it comes to saddle fitting. If the horse has well-developed withers, with good muscle cover and ribs that swell out beneath, this will make it easier for him to support the weight of a saddle and rider.

Can he 'bascule'?

People often describe the horse's outline when jumping as forming a curve or bascule. This is true, but the curvature occurs from the shoulders forward through the neck, and from the sacroiliac region backwards. The mid-back under the saddle moves very little.

Loins

The loins are not well supported by the horse's internal structures, and so are not up to carrying weight. This area is suspended between the pelvic girdle and the ribcage, and has a web of short muscles that help keep the body stable. On top of these are the long muscles of the back above and below the spine.

All these muscles are involved in movement and flexibility, and are not designed for carrying weight. It is worth noting that the major hindlimb muscles that help with movement are attached to the pelvis, not the spine.

Legs

The movement of the various joints in the fore- and hindlimbs is demonstrated clearly by this horse in piaffe.

Your horse's legs do more than hold him up, so it is a good idea to know how they work. Understanding this will help you spot problems early and enable you to create a suitable training programme for your horse.

The legs' main tasks are to support your horse's body and help him move. The limbs themselves are not simply columns of bone, but many individual bones stacked at unstable angles. Tendons and ligaments hold these bones together around the joints, helping the horse to move but limiting the movement of individual joints.

The action of muscles on joints below the knee and hock is achieved through tendons inserting into the pastern bones below the fetlock. All these parts are unstable, so it is a very sophisticated process that gets them working together – and this has to happen even when the horse is standing still.

The general functions of bones, muscles, tendons and ligaments are described on pages 13–21. Here are some important points that relate specifically to the horse's legs.

Did you know?

Only the hindlimbs are attached by bone to the rest of the horse's skeleton – the forelegs are attached by muscle and connective tissue.

The heat effect

Heat is a side effect of the cycle of loading, stretching and recoil, and is normal. However, overheating can be caused by overloading the tendon – for instance, if you make your horse do a level of work that is greater than his level of fitness, such as going from resting to cantering on hard ground too soon. The muscles may be ready, but it takes the tendons one month longer to catch up. If this happens the tendons can rupture, and behave like a piece of elastic that has lost its stretch.

Energy storage

The way the horse has evolved has resulted in all the muscles involved in leg movement being situated at the upper part of the leg, with the lower leg and foot being moved by tendons and ligaments, structures that are much less elastic. These structures store energy during the 'stance phase' (when the hoof is in contact with the ground), when they are extended to their maximum: it is at this point that all the power and thrust is generated. They return the energy to the leg at toe-off during the 'swing phase' (when the hoof has left the ground): no power can be generated during this phase.

Forelimb muscles

Joining the front legs to the spine and head is a cradle of muscles slung around the ribcage. These act to lift the ribcage between the legs, to pull the ribs on to one or other leg (for example, so that you can lift the other leg to pick out a foot), and to compensate for any discomfort in one or other limb.

A horse with a long stride length has a shoulder that moves freely, with the elbow clearing the ribcage and correct muscle action around the shoulder and the humerus, which is the foreleg bone between the shoulder joint and elbow joint.

Hindlimb muscles

The hindlimb is attached to the spine at the hip joint, which means that the hindquarters can be rotated well underneath the horse.

Most of the powerful muscles of the hindlimbs are associated with the pelvis and the femur and tibia. As we have seen, these muscles are used to generate power while the limb is in contact with the ground.

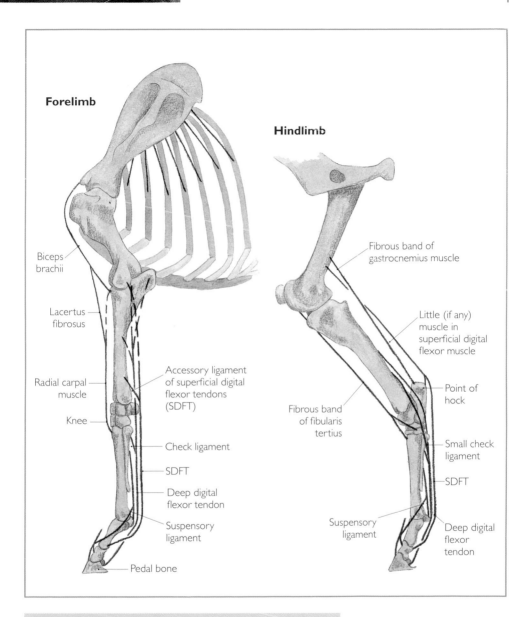

Forelimb

Hindlimb

Fibrous band of
gastrocnemius muscle

Biceps
brachii

Little (if any)
muscle in
superficial digital
flexor muscle

Lacertus
fibrosus

Accessory ligament
of superficial digital
flexor tendons
(SDFT)

Point of
hock

Radial carpal
muscle

Fibrous band
of fibularis
tertius

Knee

Small check
ligament

Check ligament

SDFT

SDFT

Deep digital
flexor tendon

Suspensory
ligament

Suspensory
ligament

Deep digital
flexor
tendon

Pedal bone

Concussion

When a horse's front hoof 'bounces' on impact it causes concussion, something that affects all the joints above it. Less concussion occurs in the hindlimbs, as the hind foot 'slides' more when it impacts the ground and more weight is carried on the forehand. In sports horses, forelimb lameness is more common than hind by a factor of 3:1, and 95% of these occur at the level of the knee or below.

Feet

The hoof plays a vital role as a shock absorber and protector of the complex internal structures of the foot – arguably it is the horse's most valuable asset.

This relatively small structure is incredibly strong and the hoof's flexibility, together with its internal structures, allows it to absorb the concussive forces of the horse's movement. With such a tiny and intricate part of the body taking so much constant pressure, it is no surprise that 50% of all lameness occurs in the foot.

To give your horse the best care possible, you need to understand how his foot is constructed. Put simply, the hoof is a hard, horny capsule that fits over the pedal bone, navicular bone and lower part of the short pastern bone.

Structure of the hoof

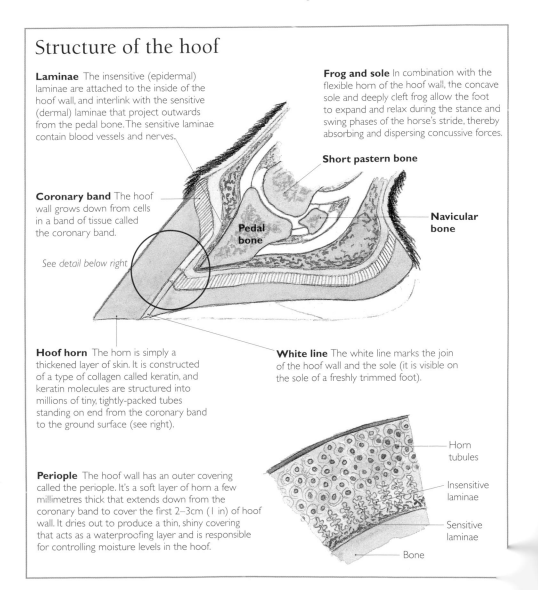

Laminae The insensitive (epidermal) laminae are attached to the inside of the hoof wall, and interlink with the sensitive (dermal) laminae that project outwards from the pedal bone. The sensitive laminae contain blood vessels and nerves.

Frog and sole In combination with the flexible horn of the hoof wall, the concave sole and deeply cleft frog allow the foot to expand and relax during the stance and swing phases of the horse's stride, thereby absorbing and dispersing concussive forces.

Short pastern bone

Coronary band The hoof wall grows down from cells in a band of tissue called the coronary band.

See detail below right

Pedal bone

Navicular bone

Hoof horn The horn is simply a thickened layer of skin. It is constructed of a type of collagen called keratin, and keratin molecules are structured into millions of tiny, tightly-packed tubes standing on end from the coronary band to the ground surface (see right).

White line The white line marks the join of the hoof wall and the sole (it is visible on the sole of a freshly trimmed foot).

Periople The hoof wall has an outer covering called the periople. It's a soft layer of horn a few millimetres thick that extends down from the coronary band to cover the first 2–3cm (1 in) of hoof wall. It dries out to produce a thin, shiny covering that acts as a waterproofing layer and is responsible for controlling moisture levels in the hoof.

Horn tubules

Insensitive laminae

Sensitive laminae

Bone

2 Preventative care

Prevention is always better than cure, particularly when it comes to maintaining soundness in your horse. This section provides details of the many steps you can take on a daily basis to ensure your horse lives a long, happy and healthy life, and that both you and he can get maximum enjoyment from the work you do together.

In this section

Keeping teeth healthy

Horse owners and riders are becoming far more clued-up about the importance of regular dental check-ups for their horses by a qualified equine dental technician (EDT) or vet. What we perhaps don't think about is the period between dental checks when, as with our own teeth, problems can arise unexpectedly.

Recognizing when dental attention is needed is half the battle, so being familiar with your horse's day-to-day foibles is the key to keeping on top of the situation. However, there are not always obvious indications that a horse needs dental attention, and some horses suffer dreadfully without any visible signs of a problem. This is why it is so important to have your horse's teeth checked every six months. In between times, keep an eye out for any of the signs listed on page 65 that may indicate there is trouble brewing.

Early warning

A vet or EDT should be able to recognize any congenital defects in the first 18 months of your horse's life – at that stage it may not be too late to correct them.

Feed naturally

It is best to feed your horse at floor level, rather than providing haynets or racks and waist-high mangers. This way, his jaws and teeth will be aligned as nature intended. You should also provide adequate (preferably ad-lib) forage, to satisfy his psychological

It is best to feed your horse both his concentrates and hay or haylage at floor level.

Receding gums

Old age and certain diseases can result in receding gums and a condition known as periodontal pocketing. The underlying area at the base of the tooth is exposed and the gum surrounding the tooth gapes, forming 'pockets' where food can collect. Bacteria thrive here, causing infection and further damage.

Following diagnosis by a vet or qualified EDT and a demonstration of the technique, you can treat this condition yourself. It involves the gentle use of a simple dental tool to remove the deposits from the gum line on a regular basis.

and physiological need to chew (see pages 9–11). If your horse makes a mess of his hay when it is fed on the floor, try a big builder's bucket and feed from that, but secure it at the sides.

Sweet tooth

Sweet treats are as detrimental to a horse's dental health as they are to ours. In fact, it is worse for horses as they can't clean their own teeth. It is probably best to cut out sweet treats entirely and substitute them with root vegetables or low-sugar treats specifically designed for horses. It is also a good idea to speak to an equine nutritionist about choosing a balanced diet and a feed low in sugars that might suit your horse better.

Plaque prevention

Preventing the build-up of plaque and keeping teeth clean and fresh on a day-to-day basis is vital to your horse's oral health.

You can now buy horse chews that are designed to help keep teeth clean and healthy. The hard, crisp texture acts like a toothbrush would, and ingredients such as mint help to combat inflammation of the gums. Chews work best where they come into direct contact with teeth, acting mainly on the molars as these teeth grind.

Alternatively, you can use a very soft toothbrush with an animal toothpaste, or tiny dab of herbal (non-fluoride) toothpaste, to brush your horse's teeth gently – if he will let you!

Chews act like a toothbrush, their texture helping to keep your horse's teeth clean.

Routine rasping

One of the most common conditions seen in horses is over-sharp teeth, or teeth with hooks. These sharp edges or points cut into the gum and cheeks, causing sores and pain to the tongue, gums and particularly the cheeks. If you notice sores on either side of the tongue, rasping (floating) is well overdue.

Rasping is a job for a vet or EDT. Apart from the obvious benefits, rasping may help the fit of the bit: rounding the front of the second premolar allows the bit to sit more easily.

The procedure is straightforward in most horses and usually takes between 10 and 20 minutes. A few animals require sedation. Larger dental spikes or hooks may need to be cut with a pair of dental shears. Carried out on a once- or twice-yearly basis, rasping will help to reduce long-term dental problems. It is also a chance to check for cracks, fractures and decay.

Take care

It is advisable to call a vet or EDT if you think the inside of your horse's mouth needs examining. As we all know, a horse's mouth can be unsafe territory, and accidents can and do happen.

The older horse

The average lifespan of the domestic horse is 25 years compared to 16 years for his wild cousin. The downfall of the wild horse is usually his teeth.

When you are trying to keep an older horse in good health, looking after his teeth is a good place to start. As a horse ages, his teeth can break, become overlong or worn down, and may even fall out. Keep up his twice-yearly dental checks, so that any problems can be dealt with as quickly as possible. Between visits, take extra care to check your horse's mouth, gums and teeth for signs of discomfort and watch for any problems with eating or drinking (see page 65), or any signs of loss of condition.

Your vet or EDT will use a variety of rasps and other tools to carry out dental procedures.

Many horses accept teeth rasping well.

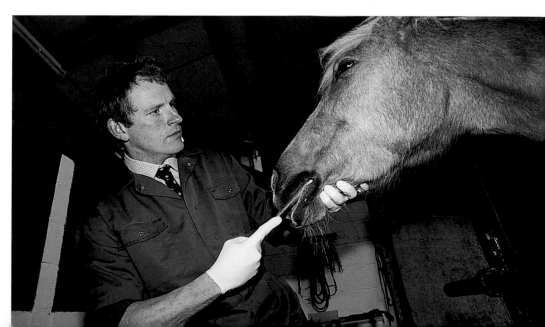

Caring for your
horse's feet

Caring for your horse's feet should be high on your list of priorities. Ensuring their good general health is a complex task, including some factors that you can't influence, such as breed characteristics and parentage. There are, however, many factors you can influence, such as stable routine and farriery. This careful management can never start too soon – even foals benefit from a good daily hoof care routine. Never forget the importance of good hoof management and, if you want the best performance from your horse, keep his feet in top condition.

Factors affecting hoof quality

The shape and strength of your horse's hooves is very important. Good feet will resist the effects of the surface you ride on, but minor knocks are cumulative and when problems arise they take most owners by surprise. Always remember that all the feet experience the same environment, so a problem will often manifest itself in more than one foot at the same time. The front feet are particularly vulnerable because they support more of the bodyweight than the hind feet and are therefore subjected to greater mechanical stresses.

Breeding

Feet vary hugely between different types of horses. Thoroughbreds, for example, are renowned for slow horn growth rates and relatively thin-walled hoof capsules, which predispose them to injuries under the stress of training. If your horse has typical Thoroughbred-type feet, you must take extra care and consider the surface you ride on when out hacking. If in doubt, discuss the quality of your horse's feet with your farrier and ask him for his recommendations.

Diet

Your horse's diet greatly influences horn quality and growth rate, which is well demonstrated by the ridges seen on hoof walls (known as grass rings) corresponding to changes in levels of nutrition. The major dietary components influencing hoof quality

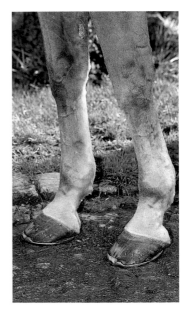

Relatively flat feet like these are more sensitive and prone to injuries and weaknesses.

Making comparisons

Good hoof management starts with good, regular farriery. This is determined by hoof growth, not shoe wear. Ask your farrier for his recommended shoeing interval and try not to exceed it. Compare the shape, size and angles of your horse's feet with those of your friends' horses and try to learn what the ideal shape is for a hoof.

Ask your vet and farrier how your horse compares with the ideal, and use this as a benchmark. You will then be better able to discuss your horse's feet with the farrier and have an influence on the type of shoe fitted.

If your horse has good feet and is ridden only lightly with little roadwork, he may be better off without shoes. You will need to discuss this with your farrier.

Clean compressed mud and/or bedding from your horse's hooves regularly and check the feet for any signs of problems.

are calcium, zinc, methionine, biotin and sulphur, which are usually found in adequate levels in good compound feeds. It is important to note that once horn has been formed nothing can be done to enhance its quality.

To help keep your horse's hooves healthy all year round, make sure he has a balanced diet. In summer, the vast majority of horses live on grass alone, but the grazing may be lacking in essential vitamins and minerals vital for healthy hooves. Give your horse a vitamin and mineral supplement every day to ensure he is getting all he needs. Specialist hoof supplements are also available – look for the key ingredients biotin and methionine, both of which are essential for strong hooves.

Environmental conditions

The weather can also affect hoof quality. Long dry spells can lead to dry, cracked hooves and wet spells can soften the horn (see opposite).

Routine management

A good stable routine is vital and should include picking out your horse's feet twice daily to remove compressed mud and manure. This is important because the ammonia in manure and urine is harmful to horn, causing it to soften and deteriorate. Poor foot hygiene can also lead to bacterial infections such as thrush. The importance of keeping the bedding clean is therefore self-evident. The type of bedding can also play a part and horse owners now use quite a wide range of materials, from plain rubber floors with no bedding to cardboard chips.

Traditional clean wheat straw still makes an excellent bedding for horses, allowing for the limitations of respiratory problems. A good alternative, which causes fewer respiratory problems, is oat straw. This tends to be quite long and much less contaminated by moulds than the other straws. Wood shavings are widely used, but they have a tendency to ball up in the horse's feet, which can cause problems if they are not picked out regularly. Shavings also tend to heat up when contaminated by manure and urine and this has the effect of drying out the feet.

Soil left in the soles and frog clefts contains countless bacteria and fungi as well as water, and if not removed will also lead to problems. Field-kept horses should have their feet picked out as regularly as stabled ones.

Moisture in the hoof

Water evaporates constantly from the outer surface of the hoof and, in order to maintain an ideal balance, it must be replaced constantly. Water is transferred from the extensive blood and lymph supply in the sensitive structures of the foot: this explains why, even in the desert where there is no external water, horses' hooves still function well.

Excess water causes the hoof wall to become soft and pliable – rather like when you have been in the bath too long and your fingernails go soft and squishy – but it does recover. However, constant overhydration caused by daily turnout in waterlogged paddocks is not good for the hoof. If the hoof is pliable and is not gradually transferring concussive forces to the inner structures of the foot, as it is designed to do, these forces could be directly transmitted to the laminae and inner structures of the hoof, leading to stretching and possible infection of the white line.

Enlarged nail holes are an open invitation to bacteria to enter and cause infection.

In hydrated hooves you can almost see the fibrous structure and the horn surface looks rougher than that of a dry foot. The area immediately below the coronary band appears white.

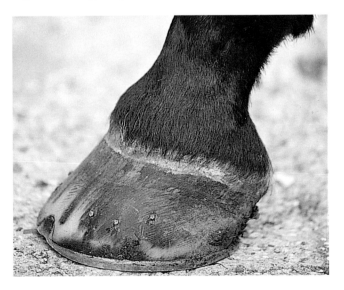

Fairly dehydrated hooves (about 25% moisture) are actually quite healthy and strong. They look dry, hard and dense .

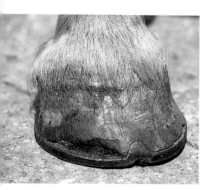

When cracks appear or the hoof starts to crumble, the damage has been done. This is a sign of hooves that have dried out quickly, been unable to cope with concussion, or have been subjected to bacterial invasion.

Top tip

Only apply protective barrier products to clean, dry hooves. If feet are wet and dirty the dressing will seal in moisture and dirt, providing an ideal environment for bacteria.

The good news is that strong, healthy hooves don't take on water very easily. Damaged hooves are much more susceptible to water absorption, as it makes its way in through cracks, splits and enlarged nail holes. However, water alone is probably a minor problem: research has shown that a mixture of ammonia and urea (from faeces and urine) has a dramatic effect on the strength of hoof horn, predisposing feet to weakness and cracks. To add to the problem, mineral salts present in muddy paddocks can also potentially disrupt keratin. Bacteria are also very bad news for feet, entering through small cracks and enlarged nail holes and causing infection, such as seedy toe and white line disease.

Stabilizing moisture content

It is rapid fluctuations in moisture that can lead to damaged hooves. Topical products may help stabilize the moisture content in your horse's hooves.

Products are available that form a one-way barrier to protect hooves in wet, muddy fields or stabled conditions from excessive absorption of water and urine. Look out for those containing antibacterial agents to guard against infection.

Hoof moisturizers are also available. Although it is not proven that these can repair already cracked feet, they might play a role in stabilizing the moisture content of hooves that are exposed to frequently changing conditions.

Working with your farrier

Having your horse shod every six to eight weeks allows your farrier to become a regular feature in your horse care routine. But what should you expect from your farrier, and what does he need from you?

What should you expect from your farrier?

It is your farrier's duty to produce a well-shod horse. This means:

■ Providing shoes of the correct weight and size, and shaping the shoe to fit the foot.

- Levelling feet and working towards correct limb alignment for easy movement.
- Ensuring there is no loss of foot bearing surface.
- Leaving the clenches even, smooth and trimmed into the hoof wall.

When dealing with your horse, the farrier should handle him in a kind but determined manner. If your horse is a bit uneasy about having his feet done, then the way in which the horse is managed should be decided between you and your farrier. If for any reason your horse needs medication to make him calm enough to shoe, the farrier should recommend that a vet be present and should not be expected to prescribe or predict what effect the medication will have on your horse.

What should your farrier expect from you?

As the horse's owner, it is your responsibility to make sure he receives quality hoof care continuously. This includes correct feeding, picking out the hooves, and teaching your horse to stand and let his feet be picked up.

It also includes making life as easy as possible for you farrier. You should:

- Make regular appointments so that your horse's feet are in the best condition possible.
- Make an appointment in advance. Your farrier has other clients to attend to.
- Provide a dry, tidy and light area for him to work in. The floor should also be hard and level. If possible, provide an area under cover if the weather is bad.
- Have your horse ready for the farrier's visit. It is not the farrier's duty to bring him in from the field and tidy his feet and legs.
- Ensure your horse is settled and ready to have his feet shod. Once your horse is ready for the farrier he should be tied in a safe manner. His headcollar should be in good condition, fit correctly and have a good length lead rope attached. It is your responsibility to provide competent assistance while your horse is being shod.

3 steps to good feet

1 Farriery

Make sure your horse has regular attention from a good farrier. Do not let his feet overgrow his shoes as this leads to cracks and enlarged nail holes through which bacteria may enter.

2 Stabilize moisture content

If your horse already has cracked or damaged hooves, avoid exposing him to waterlogged conditions. Use hoofcare products where appropriate.

3 Hygiene

Bacteria are a real problem for hooves, so help to keep them at bay by picking out hooves twice a day. If your horse is stabled, keep his bed clean and dry.

Buying a saddle is a big investment and fitting it correctly is essential in order for your horse to work easily, as any restriction could lead to problems in his back and elsewhere. It is also vital to check the saddle regularly to make sure that it is still comfortable for your horse.

Flocking Run your hands down the panels on the underside of the saddle. They should feel smooth, with no lumps or hard areas. Check also that the saddle appears symmetrical.

Pommel clearance If your horse's saddle fits correctly, you should be able to place three fingers between the pommel and his withers. If you can fit in more than this, it could mean that your saddle is too narrow. If the

pommel is sitting very low, it could indicate that your saddle is too wide or needs reflocking.

Back contact When the girth is fastened, the whole length of the saddle should be in contact with the horse's back. From behind, look along the gullet to check that the saddle sits symmetrically on his back and is not twisted. If the back of the saddle lifts up when you are riding, it may be too narrow.

Down the shoulder Place your hand flat under the front of the saddle at your horse's withers and run it down the front edge of the saddle at his shoulder. Your fingers should run easily and it should not feel tight.

Seat If the seat is not horizontal (parallel to the ground), it may be throwing you forwards or tipping you backwards. This can cause pressure on your horse's withers or loins.

Numnah Don't just check your saddle: pay attention to the fit of your numnah as well. It must be big enough and sit high enough into the gullet of the saddle so that it does not create any pressure on your horse's withers or back.

Lumps and rubs Each time you remove your saddle, check for any signs of rubbing. This could indicate that the saddle is moving or that the numnah is causing problems. Also check for lumps. These could mean that your saddle is causing pressure points and needs to be looked at by a professional saddle fitter.

Tree If the pommel of your saddle suddenly drops, check the tree. Pull the pommel and cantle towards each other: there should be some give. If there is a lot of movement, don't use the saddle and seek the advice of a professional saddle fitter.

Changes in behaviour or condition

Your horse will change shape according to his fitness, the time of year and his age. Get your saddle checked as his shape changes to ensure a good fit.

If your horse's behaviour changes – for example, he starts napping, bucking or refusing to jump – this could indicate that his saddle is no longer fitting very well and is causing him restriction, discomfort or even pain.

Consult a saddle fitter

If you are worried about the fit of your saddle, ask a qualified saddle fitter to check it. It is always better to be safe than sorry, as an ill-fitting saddle can cause a range of physical problems for your horse, some of which may become chronic if not attended to at an early stage.

Training and fitness

Cross-training involves using different activities to produce the best all-round, injury-free athlete. Injuries to horses during training and competing are depressingly common, but by adopting the principles of cross-training you can produce a horse with improved motivation and performances, a stronger, fitter body, and reduced risk of injury.

Specializing in a single activity tends to maximize only one or two aspects of your horse's ability. For example, working over poles and jumping grids will improve your horse's suppleness and technique over a fence, and control and balance between fences. However, if all you do is jump or ride flatwork for jumping, your horse will only develop those muscles he needs for jumping and will never achieve all-round body fitness. Ultimately, your horse's body may not be able to cope with the repetitive stresses involved in jumping, and he could incur injuries which result in time off work. This is no fun for you or your horse.

Riders who cross-train their horses have a great deal of fun. Their horses are willing and interested every time they are worked, and they are good all-round performers. Not only is the risk of injury to the horses reduced, the horses perform even better in the rider's preferred activity.

There are three areas to consider when producing your horse as an all-round athlete:
- Working the muscles and heart.
- Building up bone and tendon strength.
- Educating your horse and improving his flexibility.

Muscles and heart

The muscles and heart adapt fairly quickly and retain fitness for up to two weeks without training. Your horse's fitness will increase with a gradual build-up of regular hill work or short periods of fast work. Working him hard over a long period of time will tire him unnecessarily and increase his chances of injury. Instead, use short periods of uphill or fast work, interspersed with short walks to allow him time to recover.

Vary the activity

There is a variety of activities you can undertake with your horse, including:
- Lungeing or long-reining.
- Flatwork.
- Jumping.
- Roadwork.
- Riding on bridleways and tracks.
- Hill work.
- Fast work.

Use short periods of uphill work to develop fitness.

Roadwork

Gone are the days when it was thought that you had to trot for hours on the roads to harden a horse's legs. It is now known that prolonged periods of fast work on hard surfaces can result in splints, jarring and even laminitis. Slow, steady roadwork in small amounts is a useful exercise for strengthening the limbs and improving fitness, but care needs to be taken to avoid doing too much and thereby making the horse sore.

Roadwork provides a means of conditioning a horse's bones and tendons gradually. If a horse is very young or has had a long lay-off, it is a good idea to do about six weeks of slow work on the roads before starting any schooling. This should be carried out mostly at a good walk, with slow trotting preferably uphill rather than on the level to encourage the horse to push from behind and strengthen his topline. Never trot downhill on the roads as this can jar the shoulders and concuss the feet.

Bone and tendon strength

The bones and tendons take two years of consistent and progressive training to reach optimal strength. Studies have shown that the temperature inside the tendons reaches over 44°C (111°F) during exercise, and that ridden horses experience some cellular changes to central fibres in the tendons. This can damage the tendons if the correct fittening work is not carried out to strengthen them.

Hacking on roads and bridleways gives you the opportunity to develop bone strength. Long periods trotting on roads or hard ground will result in concussion to your horse's limbs, so use predominantly walking exercise to stimulate the bones to harden.

Working over a variety of surfaces (from roads or stony tracks to rough or soft, muddy going) is good for developing overall tendon strength and elasticity. Roadwork produces stiffer, stronger tendons. Rough, uneven ground causes slight twisting of the limbs, which stimulates the tendons to adapt to different strains. The effort of pulling the limbs out of soft going encourages elasticity and overall fitness in the tendons.

Too much roadwork will result in your horse's tendons not being flexible enough to cope with soft going. Similarly, working on soft going every day will not develop your horse's bone and tendon strength on harder ground, and may result in tendon strain. You should therefore try to hack out along routes which give you a combination of roadwork, tracks and softer ground in order to increase your horse's bone and tendon strength gradually without overstressing him.

Education and flexibility

Schooling your horse in an arena develops flexibility and suppleness, and educates him to your aids. You can teach him to move correctly and develop lateral work or jumping.

Vary your schooling programme to develop your horse's flexibility and suppleness by including pole work, lateral exercises and lungeing or long-reining each week. Try to include new exercises or work to improve movements that your horse finds mentally challenging.

To cross-train effectively, focus on doing several different activities each week. Decide when you will be training for bone and tendon strength, when you want to concentrate on flexibility, suppleness and educating your horse, and when you will be doing fitness work for the muscles, heart and lungs. Build up the time you spend on each of your cross-training activities so your horse has a chance to adapt to the changes in his exercise regime.

Long-reining and lungeing will add another dimension to your horse's training.

Golden rules of cross-training

1 Do not increase the amount of time you spend riding your horse. Change his weekly schedule to include cross-training activities, rather than adding them on as extra work.

2 Rest is as important as work. Make sure your horse has at least one day off per week and try to plan your cross-training so that he has an easy day after a hard day's work (for example, walking on roads and bridleways after a day of jumping, hill work or fast work).

3 Concentrate on the weaker areas. If your horse is not giving his best performance in the dressage arena and you have noticed he is flagging when you ask him to work uphill, it is possible that he needs to develop greater muscle strength in order to perform to the best of his ability. If this is the case, focus on developing your horse's muscle strength within your cross-training schedule until his dressage performance improves.

4 Think about how you can vary your training and competing. Introduce your horse to new experiences, both in his training and at competitions, to stimulate his interest.

5 Set objectives and record your progress.

Top tip

If you are using a stethoscope, count the number of heartbeats over 15 seconds and then multiply by four to get the number of beats per minute.

Your horse's pulse rate is one indication of his fitness.

How fit is your horse?

A fit horse is capable of carrying out the demands placed upon him, whatever the discipline. If you can monitor how fit your horse is throughout the year, you can tailor your riding programme to suit you both and it will enable you to get the most out of the partnership. Monitoring the fitness and general health of your horse will also mean you can spot signs of illness or injury earlier and deal with them before problems worsen.

There are several measurements you can take to assess your horse's fitness. However, it is important to remember that each horse is an individual, so you should make sure you are familiar with your horse's normal readings.

Pulse rate

Taking the pulse (number of heartbeats over one minute) is the best way to monitor your horse's immediate response to his exercise programme. Using either a stethoscope or heart monitor on the left side of your horse's chest, just behind the elbow, take his pulse at rest before exercise in a quiet environment. If you take the pulse rate when the horse is excited, it will be faster and not a true representation of his resting heart rate.

A normal resting pulse rate for a horse is 36–42bpm (beats per minute), although some horses have resting pulses as low as 25bpm. A high pulse rate when the horse is at rest and not excited or stimulated by seeing food, tack and so on may indicate pain or illness.

To test whether your horse is fit enough for the work you are doing, exercise him as part of your normal routine, then when you return to the stable take his pulse. It should return to around his resting rate a within a maximum of 20 minutes.

The pulse should not be over 64bpm as this indicates fatigue and a lack of fitness. A pulse rate in the high 50s should be treated as an indication that your horse has worked hard. The exception to this general rule would be on very hot, humid days when your horse's pulse will be higher if he is still hot after exercise. You can lower the pulse in these conditions by washing down with cold water over his neck, saddle area, between the hindlegs and, most importantly, the large muscle masses of the hind quarters.

If you are in the process of getting your horse fitter and want to measure his progress while out riding, you can use a heart rate monitor. During fast canter or gallop work, your horse's pulse may reach 160–180bpm but it should drop to below 120bpm within a few minutes of returning to slower work. Do not repeat the fast work until his pulse has dropped to 120bpm. Pulse rates during trot work vary considerably between individuals, so monitor your horse's normal pulse to enable you to pick up any changes that occur.

Breathing

Respiratory rates (the number of breaths taken over one minute) are slightly easier to measure than pulse rates, but are a less reliable indicator of fitness. Your horse's resting respiratory rate should be 8–12brpm (breaths per minute). To take the respiratory rate, either hold a wet hand by your horse's nose and feel the air as he breathes out, or watch his flanks moving and count each movement in and out as one breath.

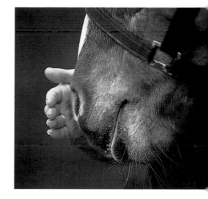

Your horse's respiratory rate is easy to measure.

Measure the respiratory rate after strenuous work such as cantering or uphill exercise to monitor your horse's fitness. Many horses will take a high number of heavy breaths immediately after hard exercise, followed by lighter breaths, and then finally the respiratory rate drops. Fitter horses will take lighter breaths and the respiratory rate will fall more quickly after exercise.

Body tone

We can all see the basic difference between a fat, unfit horse and a sleek, fit one. However, there are many levels of fitness in between these two examples. By looking at body condition and taking measurements of your horse's weight, it is possible to assess subtle changes that occur.

There are always conformational differences between horses, so get to know your horse as an individual and monitor his condition on a regular basis. (For details on weighing and condition scoring your horse, see pages 110–115.)

Competition fit?

A horse that is fit to compete in most disciplines will have:
- A level back.
- Ribs that can be felt easily (although not necessarily seen).
- Rounded withers.
- Sufficient coverage of the neck and shoulders.
- Well-covered hindquarters with the hips still able to be felt easily.

Assessing your horse

There is no such thing as 'normal' horse behaviour: what is considered the usual temperament or gait for your average cob is vastly different from that of a hot-blooded Thoroughbred. The equine species is as diverse as ours, so it is up to us to pay attention to our horses' individual quirks in order to establish what is normal behaviour for them. That way we can quickly distinguish any change from the norm and spot a potential problem before it develops into anything bigger.

What to look for

In order to spot when things are wrong with your horse, you need to know what's right. Some horses will be naturally outgoing, some more reserved, so observe your horse carefully to discover what is usual behaviour for him. Ask yourself the following questions and be observant, as any irregularities can be a sign of a more serious problem elsewhere:

Get to know your horse's character: for example, a cob's normal behaviour may be quite different to that of an Arab or Thoroughbred.

- Does your horse have clean nostrils, bright eyes and steady breathing? This is indicative of a healthy respiratory system.
- Is he happy in and around his stable? A horse that walks in and out of his stable calmly is not worried by restricted areas. If he can move around the stable easily, stand square and is happy to let you pick up his feet, this shows good posture and co-ordination. The same goes for his movements in the field: if he can step back easily to let you open a gate, then he's co-ordinated.
- Is his bedding unusually dirty, wet or disturbed? Any irregularities here can be a sign that the horse is feeling unwell. If he is drinking or staling excessively, this can mean a kidney problem, so ask your vet's advice.
- Can he roll, lie down and get up easily in the stable and the field? Any difficulties here may be indicative of a problem with mobility.
- Is he happy to graze or eat food off the floor of his stable? If he is, this shows that his teeth are working. Pain in the back can result in difficulty when eating off the floor, so watch out for signs of discomfort.

- Does your horse react calmly to being rugged up? If the answer is yes, and if his rugs usually stay in place well, this shows that he is comfortable in himself and his muscles are well balanced. If your horse tries to bite when you rug him up, this can be indicative of pain – or it could be caused by remembered pain from a past incident.
- Does your horse get on well with his field mates? A horse with psychological problems will find it difficult to mix and may be isolated from the herd, be bullied or be the bully.
- Does he move easily around the field? There should be no evidence of lameness, excessive stumbling or a reluctance to move as this can be a sign of pain. If your horse regularly pulls off a shoe in the field, this may be the result of an abnormality in his movement.

How your horse's body shapes up

Like us, horses come in all shapes and sizes, and your horse may be fit and healthy despite not conforming to the ideal look. However, it is possible to detect problems just by looking at your horse's conformation and symmetry.

Watch your horse at rest first, to judge his natural posture, then stand him square on a hard, level surface and look at him from every angle.

A lack of symmetry anywhere in the body usually indicates pain or injury, either in the past or the present. If you have a sore ankle you will shift your weight on to the other leg and horses are the same. Left unchecked, a minor muscular problem can result in a change in the way a horse carries himself and this, in turn, leads to muscle wastage. So make yourself aware of any subtle changes in your horse's movement and seek expert help to prevent long-term damage.

Check over your horse's body for signs of asymmetry and muscle wastage.

From all sides

Stand directly in front of your horse, look at his forelegs and imagine a straight line through the centre of his hoof, fetlock and knee. Check the symmetry on either side of the line and then do the same from the rear view for the hindlegs. Check for evidence of uneven wear on the shoes too. Evenly developed legs indicate that the horse is using his muscles correctly, while level, balanced legs and feet are vital for correct movement.

Next, stand on a box behind your horse, looking down on him from above. You should be able to see if his back is straight and his neck, shoulder and back muscles look the same on both sides. If he cannot stand straight, you will see uneven muscle development throughout his body.

Next, stand to the side of the horse and observe his general conformation. A good, sloping shoulder, nicely proportioned head and neck carriage, evenly muscled back and hindquarters, and sound legs and feet are all sought after. How well, or poorly, the horse moves will be evident in the shape of his topline, and if your horse has a weak conformation he will find it more difficult to carry a rider and move correctly.

On the move

You wouldn't expect an arthritic 75-year-old man to race up the stairs, and the same goes for animals. As horses age they become less mobile, so bear this in mind when you are riding and handling veteran equines. Whatever your horse's age, however, you can get a feel for how mobile he is by working him in-hand. Choose a hard, level surface and allow yourself plenty of room. Here's what to look for:

Observe your horse's movement as he walks and trots in hand.

In walk and trot

- A level, even, rhythmical stride and footfall, with good bending of the knee and hock joints. This shows effective body control, balanced feet and free movement. The neck should be relaxed and mobile in walk and level in trot. If the horse's head bobs up or down excessively, this is a sign of lameness.

- The horse should move forward actively and the walk-to-trot and trot-to-walk transitions should be balanced. Any jerking, jarring or stiffness during walk, trot or transitions can be indicative of pain or injury.

Causes of crookedness

- The horse may have had a fall some time ago and injured himself, then becoming crooked as a way to avoid using a painful part of his body.
- Teeth problems that are not attended to can result in an uneven rein contact, then asymmetry throughout the horse.
- If the rider has a crookedness that has developed over years of bad posture, this can be transferred to the horse.
- A saddle that is twisted or unevenly flocked can cause the rider to sit over to one side, resulting in an asymmetric horse.
- Incorrect shoeing can cause crookedness and imbalance in the horse.

- Each hindquarter should rise and fall evenly and smoothly (this is a sign of good mobility), and the tail should be held centrally and swing from side to side in time with the movement. If the tail is rigid or set to the side, this can be indicative of a spinal problem.
- The horse should track up (in a supple horse, the hind hooves will land in the imprint made by the front hooves).

While turning and walking backwards

- Stand just behind your horse's shoulder (three-quarters on) and ask him to turn his head and neck towards you, so that he bends from the top part of his neck. Any stiffness here can be indicative of a problem in the spine or soft tissue of the neck.
- Ask the horse to walk around you in a 5m circle to test his co-ordination and flexibility. He should take an active step with his outside foreleg and be able to bend laterally through his body. His hindlegs should cross over, with the outside hindleg actively flexing and the weight being transferred smoothly across the pelvic area.

  If the horse throws up his head, shows signs of stiffness or discomfort, or finds one direction easier than the other, these are all evidence of a problem which should be investigated by your vet or physiotherapist.
- Straighten up your horse and ask him to take a few steps back. The strides should remain even and level, there should be no sudden, abnormal movements in the head, neck or back area, and the horse should appear relaxed. Any problems here can be a sign of pain, stiffness, inco-ordination or a lack of spinal mobility. Again, this should be investigated by an expert.

Top tips

- Damaged, rutted ground will cause uneven weight distribution (which can lead to injury) and concussion to the legs and feet. Practise good pasture management and try to avoid turning your horse out into a poached paddock – especially in frosty conditions.

- Always make sure your horse is thoroughly warmed up before exercise and cooled down afterwards to prevent excess strain on his body.
- Take your horse's age, history and breed into consideration when you are observing his routine. An elderly cob-type will move and act far differently from a young Arab.
- It is worth noting how your horse behaves while he is being shod. Is he willing to lift his feet? Is he happy to be manipulated by the farrier? Your farrier is a valuable source of information, so ask his advice.
- If your horse gets cast, falls or bangs his head, get him checked out by a vet. He may appear to have survived unscathed, but the incident could have resulted in internal damage which, if left unchecked, might lead to a more serious problem.
- If you are worried about any aspect of your horse's behaviour, conformation or movement, contact your vet or a qualified equine physiotherapist or chiropractor for an expert opinion.

Ask your horse to move in a tight circle around you to check his co-ordination and flexibility.

Caring for an
older horse

Just as humans are living longer, so are our horses. Keeping your horse happy as he gets older involves monitoring his feeding routine, good general management and regular turnout. How a horse fares in old age is dependent on a number of factors including his previous workload, breed, conformation and overall health.

Horses are individuals: what suits one will not suit another. It may be possible that while your horse enjoys regular exercise and it helps to keep away his aches and pains, another may be quite happy being retired in the field. But whatever you do, you must remember that he is no longer young and you should expect to encounter some problems. For example, older horses are more likely to suffer from arthritis, teeth problems, hormonal conditions like Cushing's disease, and tumours of the skin and organs. While the list seems daunting, most horses can live a happy life even if they suffer from one or more of these conditions.

Regulate his temperature

In winter, a horse's digestive system is less effective and your veteran's internal heating system will not be as good as it used to be. It is therefore important to provide him with a well-fitting

An older horse will benefit from plenty of turnout in the field with his friends.

Take it easy

An older horse should be warmed up gently and thoroughly before being asked to do any work. In addition, cooling down after exercise, drying off and rugging up can all help to keep him comfortable. Your veteran's workload should be constantly assessed and adjusted and you should avoid hard, deep or uneven ground. In addition, keep your horse's weight under control to avoid putting additional stress on joints (see pages 110–115). Where necessary, adjust his feed and access to grazing.

Signs of ageing

- Dipped back and prominent withers.
- Muscle wastage and loose skin.
- Drooping bottom lip.
- Deepening depressions above the eyes.
- Patches of grey hairs on the face and body.

- Teeth falling out.
- Stiffness.
- Brittle bones.

turnout rug when he is out in the field. Check that the rug does not leak, because getting cold and wet will make him miserable and won't do his joints any good either.

Ensure that there is enough shelter for your horse to get out of the wind and rain, and when he comes in have plenty of warm, dry stable rugs to layer on for extra comfort.

It is equally important not to let your veteran overheat in very warm weather, as excessive sweating and low water intake can cause dehydration, which in turn may result in constipation and colic. Also check that he can get out of the sun and into the shade.

Laminitis

Older horses that are retired, or have a very light workload but are given access to unrestricted grazing, may be at risk of developing laminitis so take care to monitor and control his weight.

Dental care

Looking after your horse's teeth is one of the most important things you can do to keep him strong and healthy, so regular dental checks and paying close attention to his eating habits and condition at all times are even more important than when he was younger (see pages 33–35).

Feeding

As a horse ages, the population of micro-organisms in the hindgut (used for fibre digestion) becomes less effective. It is important gradually to alter your horse's diet accordingly. Older horses need quality feed with access to good grazing if they are to continue to thrive.

To help your horse's digestive system remain as effective as possible, you may consider adding probiotics to his diet. These are live microbial feed supplements that can improve the balance in the horse's gut.

Many feeds have been produced especially to cater for older horses. Most will provide all the recommended daily intake of vitamins and minerals necessary for your horse's health. Avoid hard pellets, which older horses will find more difficult to chew (although it may be possible to soak and soften them in hot water, which will make them easier to eat). However, if you think your horse is losing condition, you should contact a vet or qualified equine nutritionist to get expert advice.

Vaccinations

Reduced nutrient absorption in an older horse will cause him to lose condition, making him more susceptible to illness. Vaccinations will help to protect against infections such as equine influenza.

Hoof care

Watch out for uneven wearing of your horse's hooves or shoes. Whether he is still shod or not, get your farrier to check his feet every six to eight weeks. Regular shoeing and trimming will help to keep his hooves healthy and growing correctly.

Arthritis

A little stiffness is no reason to retire your horse – if a mature horse didn't suffer from some form of arthritis it would be very surprising. Gentle exercise can help to relieve the effects of old age and if your horse seems happy there is no need to stop his fun just yet. Cold, damp weather conditions tend to make joint problems such as arthritis worse, so make an extra effort to keep your horse warm and dry at this time.

Arthritis varies from intermittent stiffness to extreme pain and lameness. Caring for an arthritic horse should involve weight management, the right amount of turnout and exercise, and medication, depending on the advice of your vet.

Top tips

- If your older horse is sensitive on stony ground, clear any stones in his paddock.

- Check the wear on your horse's shoes – uneven wear could be indicative of a problem. If you are concerned, ask your farrier's advice.
- If your elderly horse is kept in at night, do not ride him straight from the stable. Either walk him in-hand or turn him out for 30 minutes to allow him to loosen up.
- An older horse will find it easier to school on grass than on deep sand as grass is a more stable surface, but be careful of jarring joints if the ground is hard.
- Turn your horse out as much as possible to ease stiffness.
- Ask a chartered physiotherapist to check your horse twice a year.
- Discuss your worming programme with your vet and have your horse blood tested if necessary to check that the programme is effective.

Get the best from
your vet

As a horse owner, it pays to build up a good working relationship with your vet.

First, get to know your veterinary practice. When you register your horse, go and have a chat with the staff. Ask your vet what over-the-phone information you need to give in the event of a problem. Find out what he suggests you keep in your first aid kit and what areas the practice specializes in.

If you know and trust your vet you can work with him, rather than feeling the need to seek lots of different opinions. If you are constantly questioning your vet's actions, he's probably not the right one for you.

What counts as an emergency?
- Breathing problems.
- Laminitis.
- Colic.
- Tying up (or azoturia).
- Extreme lameness.
- Broken bones.
- Cuts and other wounds vary in seriousness, but require a phone call to your vet at the very least.

What should your vet expect from you?

There are lots of commonsense steps you can take to make the relationship with your vet more efficient and effective.

First, know your horse's 'normals'. Get used to taking his temperature, pulse and respiration. If you can tell your vet over the phone 'My horse's pulse is usually 38 beats per minute but it has dropped to 32' this will help him to form a more accurate picture of what is going on and decide whether he needs to visit immediately.

Second, always liaise with your vet, as communication is key. Good communication will avoid unnecessary visits and ensure important cases are dealt with quickly and effectively. It is reasonable for your vet to expect you to give him accurate information over the phone. This includes what is wrong, the symptoms, and any changes to normal eating habits, movement and so on. If your horse is lame, rate the lameness – 0 being normal and 10 a smashed leg.

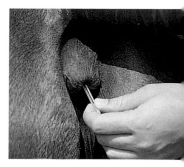

Get into the habit of recording your horse's normal temperature.

The best person to make the initial call is the person who has actually seen the horse and can accurately describe the situation. Take a deep breath, think about what you are going to say and be objective, not emotional.

If a visit is necessary, you should be there when the vet arrives, and make sure you have organized the basics he needs to work – a supply of clean water, good light and so on. You should have brought the horse in, rinsed any wounds with salt water (talk to your vet before applying anything else) and made the horse comfortable.

3 Problem solving

No matter how much time and trouble you take to provide your horse with the best possible care, it is almost inevitable that soundness problems will arise at some point. This section will help you to recognize the early signs that something may be wrong, understand the symptoms, and know when to call in your vet or other equine expert.

In this section

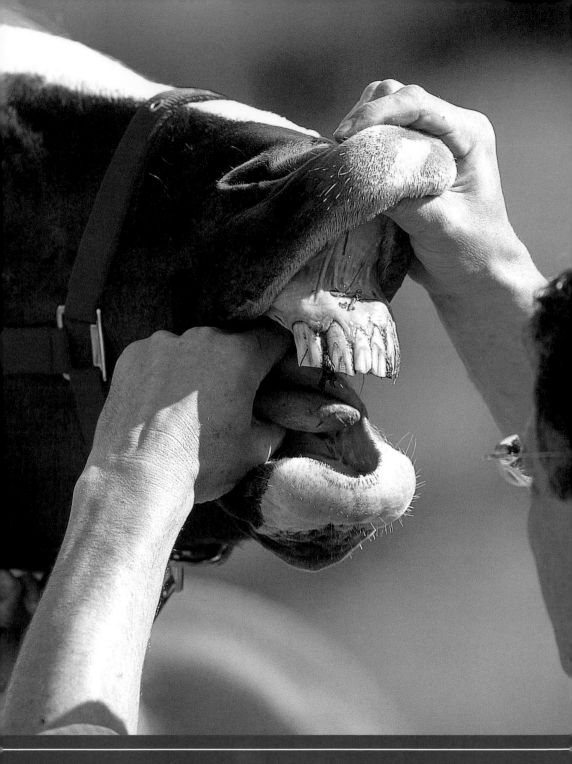

Does my horse have
teeth problems?

There are many signs of dental problems in horses. Sometimes behavioural changes may occur that do not immediately point towards difficulties with the teeth (tushes). The list is long and includes some obvious signs and others that are more obtuse:

- Dropping half-chewed food – this is sometimes referred to as quidding.
- Slower eating than normal.
- Headshaking, especially when the horse is being ridden but also while eating.
- Reluctance to respond to the bit.
- Drinking slowly – cold water on a sore tooth will amplify the pain.
- Dropping hay into the water bucket – some horses pick up on the fact that this softens the hay.
- Bad breath.
- Drooling.
- Recurrent colic or choke.
- Nasal discharge.
- Sores around the gums, tongue and lips.
- Firm swellings on the face or jaw.
- Weight loss.
- Poking the tongue out of the mouth.

If you notice any of these signs, ask your vet to take a closer look at your horse's teeth. He will question you about the background facts associated with your horse's behaviour and then look inside his mouth. The vet is checking for evidence of:

- Gum inflammation, with associated sores and ulcers.
- Wounds on the tongue.
- Sharp teeth edges and hooks.
- Cracked teeth.
- Misaligned teeth.
- Problems with wolf teeth.
- Problems with tooth eruption.
- Swellings around the face and jaw.

Teeth problems such as decay, abscesses and other infections are one possible cause of a nasal discharge.

Problems with his teeth may cause a horse to poke his tongue out of his mouth to find relief.

Abnormal wear

Irregularities in the grinding surfaces of the teeth can lead to abnormal wear. This can be caused by a variety of problems:

Missing teeth Teeth may fall out as your horse gets older, or they may need to be pulled out, or they may never grow properly. The outcome in all these cases is overgrowth in the opposing tooth. This will be picked up and managed during regular dental check-ups.

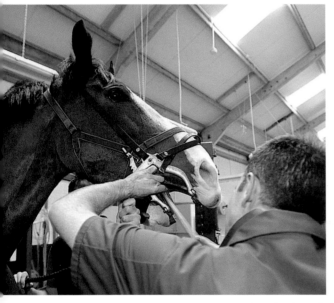

Your vet or EDT will use a gag to hold your horse's mouth open while he works.

Sharp points and hooks These are usually resolved by tooth rasping during regular dental check-ups.

Wave mouth As the name suggests, humps and troughs develop along the dental arcade leading to an undulating wave. This is more common in older horses and leads to periodontal disease.

Step mouth Missing or damaged teeth may cause overgrowth of the opposing tooth, leading to variation in the height of the teeth.

Shear mouth Exaggeration of the angle at which the molar teeth meet can inhibit the lateral movements of the jaw. Gingivitis (gum disease) and periodontal disease often follow.

Smooth mouth This condition occurs when the dental crown becomes worn away, leading to rapid wear of the root of the tooth. Prolonged periods on poor or sandy grazing lead to this condition, as do congenitally weak teeth. Weight loss will result as chewing becomes impossible.

Abnormal incisor wear This occurs in certain behavioural problems such as crib biting. It is also seen where the teeth do not quite meet correctly (for example, in parrot mouth).

Many of these conditions are not completely curable but may be controlled by good diet, regular dentistry and the resolution of problems such as crib biting. As with humans, having parents with good teeth is a bonus as the genes should pass to the offspring.

Dental caries (decay)

Decay is most frequently seen in the upper cheek teeth. Unfortunately, the early signs are not easy to spot. They become evident when the problem impacts on another organ, such as the maxillary sinus. Nasal discharge or facial swelling may be the first sign to be identified.

Dental caries are caused by a structural weakness in the tooth or teeth, which leads to formation of a pit or crevice. This fills with food, which ferments, and the resulting acids go on to dissolve the tooth. Radiographs (X-rays) may be useful to confirm the situation. In moderate cases the tooth may be flushed and filled with dental filler, but in more severe cases the tooth should be removed.

Persistent deciduous (milk) teeth

The milk teeth can act like a cap as the adult tooth emerges, causing pain, quidding and discomfort. These baby teeth should be removed, either with the fingers or using dental instruments. This can be a simple or difficult procedure, depending on which tooth is involved and the extent of the problem.

Wolf teeth

Wolf teeth are the first premolars. They are vestigial, or under-developed, teeth present in a high proportion of horses. They are usually found in the upper jaw, rarely in the lower jaw. If these teeth do not erupt they may be referred to as blind wolf teeth.

Wolf teeth can cause problems associated with the bit and a headshy horse may have difficulties associated with these teeth. They can be removed easily by a trained professional with no lasting consequences.

Canine teeth (tushes)

It is not normal for mares to develop canine teeth (tushes) as this is usually a male trait. However, around 5% of mares have these large teeth, which normally erupt when the horse is around five years old. The speed of eruption varies from horse to horse.

When the canine teeth come through, there can be a problem with the bit. The teething process is painful, as the gum over the growing tooth becomes sore. Rubbing a local anaesthetic gel (such as a teething gel designed for babies) on the gum around the emerging tooth will help soothe the pain. Once the tip of the tooth has broken through, the pain will disappear and the rest of the tooth will follow through.

Dental fractures

Teeth can easily be broken by outside trauma, perhaps from a misplaced bit or a knock. Sometimes a tooth can break due to a large cavity or an inherent weakness. Dental fractures are more common in younger horses, as their teeth are more brittle.

Minor fractures can be of no consequence, but more severe breakages may lead to the exposure of the pulp cavity, resulting in nerve pain and infection. If such teeth do not settle with simple surgical cleaning and flushing by a vet, they may need to be extracted.

Food impacted between the teeth should be flushed out regularly (see Case study).

Periodontal disease

This is caused by food impacting between the teeth (usually the cheek teeth). Dental conditions such as shear mouth or malpositioned teeth with gaps between them predispose the horse to this problem. Poor quality diets increase the chance of this situation developing. The impacted food can lead to infection, abscesses and eventual loss of the tooth. To avoid tooth removal, any impacted food must be regularly flushed away.

Case study: Fracture and infection

I would appreciate some advice on how to manage my pony's mouth problem. Eighteen months ago, during a regular dental check-up, it was discovered that he had broken off part of one of his right upper molars. The vet rasped the edges smooth and said it wasn't a bad break and advised me to keep an eye on it. I now have this tooth checked every six months as it rubs a little on the gum and causes sores.

Two months ago, my vet rasped the broken tooth again and another chunk broke off, this time with quite a lot of blood. The vet cleaned it thoroughly and showed me how to remove impacted food.

He mentioned that the tooth might have to be removed and, if this was the case, then it would be better to let it weaken itself first. My pony doesn't seem to be in pain, but it is a problem when he eats (he lifts his head and opens his mouth). What is the best way to clean this very awkward area?

Also, my pony has mild Cushing's and my vet said the crack could have occurred because Cushing's ponies can suffer from osteoporosis. Should I give him something to strengthen his bones and teeth? Should I try to disinfect his mouth after eating, and is the tooth likely to cause dental disease, or to affect his sinuses and surrounding bone?

Here are the answers to your questions, in the order you asked them:

■ If your pony will stand for this, the simplest way to clean the broken tooth and cavity is to put a moderately fast-running hosepipe into his mouth and let him play with the water. This easy method works well on a daily basis. However, some horses will not tolerate this. Another solution is to purchase a good quality gag from your vet. Unfortunately, these can be expensive, but are vital to allow you to clean out the area safely with your fingers. Teeth are formed early on in a horse's life and are not subject to calcium removal. Calcium supplementation would not be useful.

■ If you can adequately flush and clear the area with water, disinfection is not necessary.

■ Local infection around the remaining tooth is likely. The infection can occur either around the sides of the tooth or in the centre. Both types will loosen the tooth over time.

■ The way the infection manifests itself depends on which tooth is affected. The first three molars from the front of the mouth have roots embedded in the bone of the skull: infection appears as swelling over the tooth on the outside of the face, as the surrounding bone is affected. Sometimes an infected tract will burst out on the side of the face. The last three molars have roots poking into the sinuses: an infection will manifest itself with little or no facial swelling, although there is often a nasal discharge representing the overflow of pus from the sinus into the nasal passage. If a tooth becomes infected it rarely leads to damage to the neighbouring teeth.

■ The remains of your pony's tooth may need to be removed. If so, check if an intra-oral approach and removal (via the mouth) is possible, either with your pony standing or under anaesthesia. An X-ray of the tooth area will give your vet a better idea as to how feasible this is.

■ If this is not possible, a larger and more complex operation will be necessary. This would involve the tooth being approached from the side or the top in the case of the first three molars; or, in the case of the last three molars, being removed through a hole made in the sinus on the side of the pony's face. You should consult your vet and discuss all the possible complications.

Older horses are more susceptible to food impaction, as their teeth gradually wear out and they are unable to chew fibrous material efficiently. In severe cases, short chops that can be used as hay replacers are still too long. In these cases, a high-fibre cube can be soaked to create a mash that is easy to chew.

Tooth abscess

Bacterial infection may occur at the top of any tooth, resulting in swelling of the face or lower jaw. There may be nasal discharge, plus discharge from the lower jaw, depending on the tooth involved. Abscesses are often due to overcrowding and impaction. They can also arise from retained milk teeth or from infections spreading from elsewhere in the body. Horses up to five years old are particularly susceptible.

Many tooth abscesses resolve with time and appropriate antibiotic therapy. Failing that, X-rays may lead to surgical scraping and flushing by a vet. If all measures fail, the tooth may ultimately need to be removed.

Tongue ulcers

The most common cause of ulceration to the tongue is sharp teeth, which is one of the reasons why it is important to have your horses' teeth checked regularly. Another possible cause is Cushing's, as oral ulceration can be a feature of this disease, so checking for other signs (such as weight loss) is important.

If several horses on the same pasture are affected, it is more likely that the problem has been caused by something they have come into oral contact with. This could be anything from a poisonous plant to a mildly toxic chemical, or even very coarse hay. Topical applications to the tongue and mouth are usually ineffective, so the main priority is to remove the cause.

A balanced diet is also important, particularly for older horses, whose digestive systems may not be so efficient, as a reduction in the absorption of key nutrients may lead to ulcers.

Providing minerals

A mineralized salt lick is a useful way of allowing a horse to top up on any minerals he may be short of, which can be a cause of ulcers. However, if several horses are sharing the lick it is important to check that they are all using it. To provide vitamins that may not be present in the lick, a low-calorie feed balancer would help to ensure that the horses receive the key nutrients they need in a concentrated form.

Dentigenous cyst

These are rather peculiar and unusual cysts containing embryonic tooth or other fragments. They exist away from the normal teeth arcades, usually showing as discharging swellings around the head in a younger horse. They are identified by X-rays and should be removed surgically by a vet.

Tumours

Very rarely, swellings around the face of a horse can turn out to be a form of cancer. Initially, they look like many other swellings. If other avenues have failed, your vet might take X-rays and perform a biopsy to be sent away for microscopic analysis. Surgery and radiotherapy are sometimes possible, but it should be stressed that oral tumours associated with the teeth are very rare.

Parrot mouth

The formation of sharp edges and points on the horse's teeth caused by his natural chewing action is further exaggerated in the case of a parrot mouth, where the teeth do not meet as they should. It is therefore very important that such a horse's teeth are checked by a vet or EDT every six months. The horse will be prone to weight loss, diarrhoea, impactions, colic or choke if appropriate dental checks are not carried out on a regular basis.

The key to feeding horses that have problems chewing is to offer them feeds that are easy to chew and digest. Cubes are a good feed, as they can be soaked in warm water to form a soft, palatable mash that is very easy to chew. Choose a feed balancer that contains yeast and a probiotic, which will help to increase the efficiency of the horse's digestion and therefore maintain condition. Adding oil to the feed helps to increase the energy density of the diet, while keeping meal sizes small. As oil is a good source of slow-release energy, it will not exaggerate the temperament of a fizzy horse.

The horse's forage ration should be very good quality. Hay should be soft, not coarse. Test this by squeezing a handful of hay hard in the hand – it should not hurt. Haylage tends to be softer and, as it generally has a higher digestible energy level in comparison to hay, will also help to put on condition. Remember, however, that haylage has a higher moisture content than hay, so you need to feed more of it to ensure the same fibre intake.

As a general rule, horses that require more condition should be fed ad-lib forage. If the horse struggles to eat enough long forage, some of the forage ration can be replaced by alternative fibre sources such as high-fibre cubes, which can be soaked and mixed with a good quality chaff.

Bitting problems

Many riders and trainers have a favourite bit or bits that they like to use on every horse. However, horses are individuals and what suits one may not suit another. In order for your horse to be happy being ridden – and for you to enjoy riding him – he needs to be comfortable with his bit.

When a horse develops a problem in his training – maybe he puts his head in the air or suddenly begins to take off at speed – it is easy to jump to the conclusion that a different bit will remedy the situation. However, this is not a decision to be taken lightly. The bit is a way of establishing or improving communication with your horse; a tool to allow you to move the horse forward in his training. Successful training is only achieved through patience and repetition, and nothing will compensate for lack of time or poor, hurried training practices. If you are thinking of changing your horse's bit for any reason, stop and think again. A new bit is not a quick fix for any situation – unless your horse's current bit is ill-fitting or causing pain – and it will not solve behavioural or schooling problems.

When you encounter a problem that you think may be to do with your horse's bit, it is first vital to establish that the cause is not something else entirely. A look at your horse's lifestyle and general comfort may help (see overleaf) and could even result in your horse becoming more willing and easier to train, without you having to invest in new gadgets.

Only when you can genuinely say that everything in your horse's life is as good as you can get it, is it time to look at whether a change of bit would help. The question you need to ask yourself is:

Is my horse's bit comfortable for him?

The structure of your horse's head and mouth is of great importance in determining how any bit will fit and work – and, of course, how comfortable your horse will be in it. Here are some of the key conformational points to consider when making your choice.

Tongue thickness

The size of the tongue has a great impact on how each bit works, as the action of most bits is divided between the tongue and the bars of the mouth. With a thick tongue, the bit will touch the bars much later; with a thin tongue, it will make contact earlier. To find out how thick your horse's tongue is, part his lips at the side, opposite the bars (with the teeth still closed). Does the

Can he swallow?

One of the most important things to understand about the relationship between the tongue and the bit is that most bits prevent the horse from swallowing easily. If you put your finger on the middle of your own tongue and press it down into your lower jaw, you will find that you cannot swallow, as you need to lift and elevate your tongue to swallow freely. The horse's mouth works in a similar way, as he twists and elevates the tongue in order to swallow.

If you use the reins only to signal and not to restrict, most horses can cope with the pressure. However, if you use the reins continuously, for example with a horse who is difficult to control or to try to maintain a head carriage, then you restrict his ability to swallow and he will resist the pressure or pain to which he is being subjected.

Check out your horse's lifestyle

Ask yourself two simple questions about your horse's regime:
- Am I giving my horse the right feed for the work he is doing?
- Does my horse spend an acceptable amount of time out of his stable each day?

Then, look at the horse himself, and ask yourself:
- Is he suited to the work I want him to do?
- Is he old enough to cope with the work I'm expecting him to do?
- Is he fit enough for the work?

And, most importantly, ask yourself about the physical issues:
- Has my horse had his teeth checked recently?

Problems in the mouth can lead to behaviour that is often interpreted as naughtiness or bolshiness when in fact the cause is pain.

If sharp edges on the teeth are neglected for a short period of time they can cause slight discomfort and some bruising – but even this is enough to result in an uncomfortable mouth for bitting purposes. If allowed to go unchecked, the tongue and cheeks can become badly bruised and cut, taking time to heal and causing serious mouth and bitting problems.

In addition to the list given on page 65, look out for these signs that your horse's teeth may need attention:

General resistance to the bit where none previously existed.

Obvious discomfort when the noseband is done up tightly (this causes the horse's cheeks to be pressed on to the sharp edges of the teeth).

Reluctance to have the sides of his face handled.

- Is my horse's back comfortable?

If you think that your horse has any discomfort in his back, get a qualified practitioner to assess him and either give him a clean bill of health or treat him and eradicate the discomfort. Ask your vet to recommend someone he approves of.

Saddles must be fitted professionally and then flocked and checked by a qualified saddle fitter on a regular basis. An uncomfortable back can lead to many problems that no bit can possibly solve. A horse will never be able to relax comfortably and lower his head to work if his saddle is causing him pain.

tongue appear to fill the mouth cavity? Does it fill or even bulge out over the bars, indicating that perhaps there isn't much room for a very thick bit or a combination of bits?

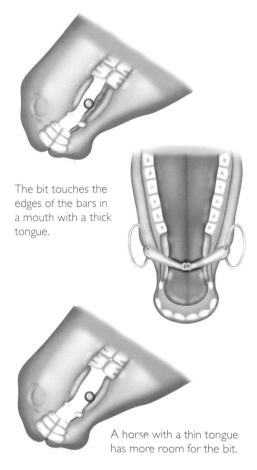

The bit touches the edges of the bars in a mouth with a thick tongue.

A horse with a thin tongue has more room for the bit.

The bit touches more of the bars in a mouth with a thin tongue.

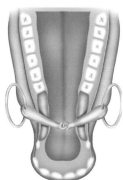

Low curb groove

The distance between the corners of the lips and curb groove is a important factor if you use, for example, a pelham. If there is quite a distance between the two, it could mean that a curb chain or leather curb strap would flip up out of the groove and put all the pressure over the very sensitive mandible nerve that runs down the back of the jaw line. In this case, a bit that doesn't have a curb chain, or a curb bit with a shorter cheek above the mouthpiece and a chain that is fixed lower on the cheek, would be the answer.

If the position of the curb groove causes the curb chain to slip upwards, it could press on the mandible nerve (shown in green).

Short mouth

Look at the length of the mouth from the lip corner to the tip of the nose. The distance may be very short, causing the centre joint of a jointed bit to hang too low, and possibly (in extreme cases) even interfere with the front teeth.

A jointed bit may hang too low in a very short mouth.

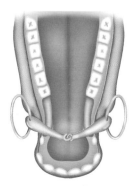

Narrow bottom jaw

Check if your horse has a narrow bottom jaw by making a fist and placing it between the rounded cheekbones under the horse's face. By checking a few horses you should be able to determine how narrow your own horse's jaw is.

Check the width of your horse's jaw by placing your fist between his jawbones.

Shallow bottom jaw

A bottom jaw with plenty of depth can accommodate the tongue, and as the horse feels pressure from the bit he can move the tongue by flattening it into the floor of the jaw. However, if your horse has a very shallow bottom jaw, a sensitive tongue has nowhere to go unless it is pulled up above or even over the bit.

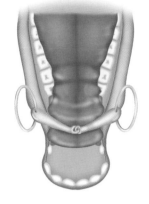

A sensitive tongue will be pulled above or over the bit if the jaw is shallow.

Low roof

A horse with a very low, sensitive roof of the mouth will not be comfortable in a port that puts too much pressure on this area. Even a single-jointed snaffle could touch the roof, so some horses may have to be bitted with very little or no pressure in this area.

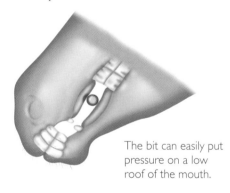

The bit can easily put pressure on a low roof of the mouth.

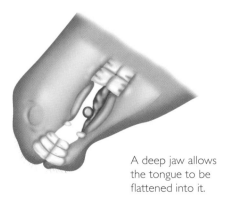

A deep jaw allows the tongue to be flattened into it.

Corners of the lips

The lip corners can very easily be made sore by overuse. Old injuries in this area also need careful consideration, as any severe use of a bit will result in a recurrence.

Fleshy lips

Very fleshy lips are difficult to accommodate and can be easily nipped or bruised by loose-ring or sliding-cheeked bits. There is less risk of this happening if the bit has eggbutt sides and fixed cheeks. A horse with fleshy lips who is bitted with a curb-chained bit can get the extra flesh caught in the curb chain hooks; in this case, a flat curb chain hook is a better alternative.

Width of face

If your horse has a triangular face (narrow at the muzzle, quickly getting wider as you look up the face), it can be difficult to use a pelham or a weymouth. You need to find a bit with a short cheek above the mouthpiece that is also curved outwards, to make sure it clears the face and doesn't rub or dig into the cheeks.

If you are in any doubt about the fit of your horse's bit, get expert help. You can try different bits through bit hire services, until you find one that really suits him.

Bitting tips

- Check your horse's face and mouth on a regular basis, so you are instantly alerted to any injury or change.
- Often, it is only when we are faced with a problem that we really begin to think about what goes on inside a horse's mouth when bit pressure is applied. However, once you begin to build up a picture of your horse's conformation and how he reacts to pressure from the bit, you can bit him for more comfort and better communication.
- Don't be tempted to look for a quick fix when it comes to bitting. Work through the questions listed above and take into account all the information about mouth and head conformation. If your horse is uncomfortable in his bit, he will try his best to tell you – and it's your job to listen, understand and make things better for him.
- A horse can communicate with us in two ways: he can be obedient and relax into his work, or he can be resistant (what we assume to be disobedient). Resistances to the bit can be mild and barely a problem, or they can be very pronounced and even dangerous. Remember that when a horse resists the action of the bit, he is simply trying to move his face in order to make the bit in his mouth more comfortable.

Headshaking

For owners of headshakers, spring is a time of dread. This is when horses that headshake start to show the distressing symptom of violently shaking their head, usually when ridden. The condition can generate apprehension in even the most experienced horsemen, as the search for effective control is often frustrating and frequently fruitless. The lack of sound, conclusive scientific studies has led to many myths surrounding this condition and it is only now that vets are beginning to get a clearer picture of what is really going on.

Headshaking comes in various forms and is associated with irritation of the horse's face. In some cases this is quite mild, perhaps being caused by poorly fitting tack. It can also be a temporary condition, such as the behaviour that occurs as the animal tries to rid himself of flying insects around the face and eyes. These problems are easily rectified.

Signs of headshaking

The real problem is a much more durable condition. The term headshaking describes a syndrome that actually includes many other behaviours – headshaking itself is just one of the most obvious and distressing aspects.

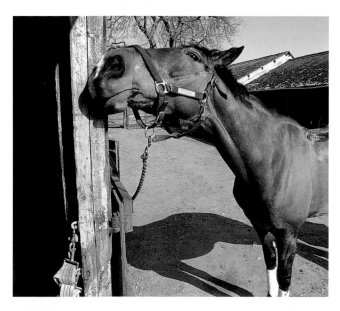

Pinpointing the problem

The occurrence of certain behavioural features may suggest irritation of a specific area.

- Flipping the nose, sneezing, snorting and clamping the nostrils as if to close them, and attempts by the horse to rub his face on a foreleg are all thought to be responses to naso-facial irritation or pain.
- Horses that shake their head horizontally, either in addition to or instead of the classical vertical movement, or rub their ears, amy be more likely to have a pain focus around the ears, such as might occur with an ear mite infestation.

Nose rubbing is just one behaviour associated with headshaking.

A typical headshaker is a horse that displays recurrent, intermittent, sudden and apparently involuntary bouts of head tossing. This may be so extreme as to throw the horse and rider off balance. The affected horse may also frequently sneeze and snort, and keep attempting to rub his nose on the ground, his forelegs or any nearby objects.

Although the condition can occur at rest, more cases are obvious during exercise, especially at trot. It can, however, be seen at any pace.

The prevalence of headshaking remains unknown, but many horses suffering from this serious problem cannot be competed or ridden safely. It may strike at any age and both yearlings and senior animals (over 20 years old) have been known to be affected for the first time. However, it seems to start most frequently in mature animals around the age of eight years.

Possible triggers

Headshaking appears to be seasonal in about 60% of cases. In about one-quarter of seasonal cases, the length of time for which the animal displays the behaviour tends to increase year on year. This pattern led some early researchers to focus their attention on summer-related problems like hayfever (allergic rhinitis) as potential causes. However, many other factors also correlate with this time of year, such as riding out and changes in light intensity, and it now seems unlikely that allergies are a common cause of headshaking.

There is no evidence of management factors – such as the bedding material used, trimming of the whiskers or diet – being important in triggering the problem. The use of the horse and the presence of respiratory allergies do not seem to increase the risk in any way either. However, conversely, headshakers may be at a greater risk of non-respiratory allergies.

In fact, more than 60 conditions have been listed in the veterinary literature as possible causes of headshaking syndrome, but vets can rarely identify a physical cause.

Susceptibility

Several studies have found that headshaking is twice as common in geldings as mares, and Thoroughbreds appear to be at greater risk of developing the behaviour, but interestingly it is rarely seen in active racehorses.

Nerve damage

Recent attention has focused on the potential role of one of the largest nerves of the head, called the trigeminal nerve. This has several branches which relay sensory information from the head, and sudden stimulation of the nerve is likely to result in reflex motor responses such as those seen in headshakers. In some cases this nerve may become diseased or damaged, causing pain to be felt in the area it serves (neuralgia), but in others the situation is more complex.

It is possible that damage to the trigeminal nerve in one region could set up painful sensations in other areas, a phenomenon known as referred pain. There are a number of places where this nerve is at greater risk of damage, so these should be of particular concern. One large branch emerges halfway down the face and could be harmed by something as simple as a badly fitting bridle or even a headcollar.

However, it has also been suggested that nerve damage could

Headshakers often show dramatic symptoms, yet the exact cause of this syndrome is still unknown.

Excess bit pressure can cause bony changes under the bars of the mouth. This jaw bone should be smooth.

occur due to a reaction to the bit in the lower jaw. Evidence has been found for bony changes occurring in this region of the mandible in many ridden horses. This theory does not discount the possible role of light as a trigger for headshaking, as light can cause a tingling sensation in this same nerve. Indeed, many people sneeze when a bright light is shone in their faces. It could be that in some horses, light makes matters worse and so although the horse is reacting to the bit, this only becomes apparent when the light is bright.

Diagnosis: full veterinary procedure

A horse may headshake for a number of reasons and it is a challenge for any vet to arrive at a correct diagnosis. Once the basics such as ear mites, teeth and mouth problems, skin conditions and eye defects are ruled out (see Case Study), it is likely that the headshaking problem is more deep-seated.

Further diagnostic procedures, involving the use of an ophthalmoscope to look into the eyes and an endoscope to view the nasal turbinates (walls of the nasal passages) and pharyngeal areas, will be carried out if no common cause can be found. If all these processes draw a blank, the vet can take X-rays to rule out sinus disorders and possible fractures of the hyoid apparatus (a bone at the base of the tongue).

If all the above prove negative, a diagnosis of trigeminal neuralgia can be made.

Gender reaction

A reaction to the bit could explain the increased risk of headshaking in males, who (unlike females) develop a lower canine tooth. The root of this tooth curves backwards and is well supplied by blood vessels and nerves, including branches of the trigeminal nerve. This gives potential for bit pressure to instigate a reaction within the nerve in males.

Treatments

The table on page 84 shows the reported success of treatments for headshaking used by a total of 245 owners consulted in one research survey. The most popular feed supplements used were herbal products such as echinacea.

While some of these methods may indeed have helped in an individual case, some of the improvements seen could have been

Case study: Diagnosis in logical steps

When I bought my mare a year ago, she frequently shook her head. Her teeth were rasped, but the shaking got worse. When ridden outside she shakes her head and refuses to go forward, but when she's inside, lunged or turned out, she's fine.

Her back and saddle have been checked and they're fine. I've tried a nose net, and a physiotherapist says she is tight in the back. We can't tell if this is because of her head or whether she tosses her head to relieve the tightness in her back. I'm worried there is some sort of physical problem that I haven't picked up.

There are several interestings things in your description of your mare. You say she only headshakes when she's outside, and works nicely indoors. My first reaction would be that if the problem were pain-related, there would be no reason why it should suddenly improve when you go indoors only to return when you go back outside. This would rule out the possibility of irritation caused by bitting problems or an ill-fitting bridle. It's also interesting that she doesn't headshake when turned out.

In these situations it is often too easy to change lots of things at once. If you do this, you won't know which change or action is giving you the result you require. Follow these steps one at a time to see if you can identify the problem.

■ Keep a daily diary – note the temperature and weather conditions, the work your mare does and her response.

■ Also note when your mare comes into season. The ovaries are found in the lumbar region, so when she ovulates this may cause the tension in her back. See if a pattern of behaviour emerges.

■ Get your vet to give her a thorough check over, including looking at her ears to check for fungal infection, mites or an inflammation, examining her mouth for sharp teeth, lacerations or ulcers, and checking for other skin conditions affecting the head.

■ Get your physiotherapist to check her again – can they cause a headshaking response by applying pressure to a tight area? Does it improve at all after the spasm is released, and how long does she remain tension-free post treatment?

■ Try to find out some history on your mare. What was she doing before you bought her? Perhaps she only hunted, so never worked in summer. Don't be afraid to ask questions to get to the bottom of it.

■ Does she try to shake her head like this with everybody? Try to get someone else to ride her and watch her response. Is she worse when asked to come on the bit?

■ Try giving her a magnesium supplement – this can sometimes work well on stress- or tension-related problems.

Having exhausted this list, you may have to try other things such as a desensitizing cream if a nose net is ineffective. There is usually a reason for this sort of behaviour, but at the end of the day you might have to accept that your mare is a true headshaker and proceed with a full veterinary diagnosis.

Other methods

The 'other methods' mentioned in the table included inhalation of friar's balsam, vinegar and oil rubbed on the muzzle before exercise, sunblock, a leather fringe on the horse's noseband, feeding only grass and hay, keeping the horse in an open barn, riding at dawn and moving the horse to another location.

Treatment	Percentage treated	Complete success %	Partial success %	No success %
Traditional vet treatment	52	6	22	72
Back specialist	21	0	8	92
Homoeopathy	38	6	31	63
Other alternative therapies	16	5	13	82
Nose veil/net	73	27	34	39
Ear net	34	4	29	67
Face net	21	8	41	51
Feed supplement	43	5	30	65
Other methods	37	11	43	46

simple coincidence. It is worth noting that trigeminal neuralgia in humans often causes unpredictable pain, but spontaneous periods of temporary relief are not uncommon. It is therefore possible that one of the reasons there are so many treatments that owners claim to be successful is because their horses happened to improve when they tried a specific treatment. However, this does not mean the treatment was the cause of the recovery: it might be that this was going to happen anyway.

Drugs can be useful in some cases, but they are expensive and not without risk. The effects are short-lived in many horses, although in others they can last for much longer. Various forms of surgery have also been attempted to destroy the nerve relaying the painful feelings. Again, this can be very useful in some cases, but it is a major undertaking that carries considerable risk. Surgery is often irreversible and any side effects (such as self-mutilation of the muzzle) may also be impossible to correct.

Nose nets

Nets reduce turbulent airflow through the horse's nose and lead to an improvement in many headshakers.

More than one-quarter of owners in the survey said they achieved complete control of the problem with a nose net, suggesting that the positive response is not coincidental.

Traditionally, nose nets have been thought to act as a filter for pollens and other items that might irritate the nose if inhaled, but a recent study has shown that equally good results may be obtained with an alternative 'half-net' with a large mesh. This suggests that nets probably do not act simply as a filter, and it now seems likely that they may work by reducing turbulent airflow through the nose, which could cause stimulation of sensitized branches of the trigeminal nerve within the nose. This may explain why the problem is more common at the trot, and possibly in dressage horses, as the angle of the head during these exercises may encourage a more turbulent airflow pattern.

Headshaking is more commonly displayed in trot, and especially in dressage horses.

It would also explain why the radical surgical procedure of tracheostomy (where a hole is created in the windpipe so that air can enter the lungs without going through the nose) appears to have a high rate of success in relieving the signs in the small number of cases on which it has been tried. While surgery in these cases may relieve the pain, there is unfortunately a serious risk of complications that compromise the welfare of the horse.

Conclusion

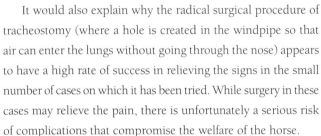

Headshaking has many causes, but with careful evaluation it may be possible to determine the root of the problem in some cases. However, it would seem that many cases reflect a hypersensitivity of one branch of the trigeminal nerve, exacerbated by environmental triggers. In these cases it is important for riders, trainers and owners to recognize that the headshaking is a response to pain and that the horse must be managed sympathetically and not simply ridden through the problem.

Research is ongoing into the root of the disease and its trigger factors (such as exposure to bright light), in the hope of developing a method of preventing the triggers from setting off the pain. Until a cure can be found or trigger factors removed, a nose net remains one of the simplest and most effective treatments.

Latest research

Some researchers have begun to suspect that the basis for headshaking is most likely laid down when the horse is a foal and is exposed to the equine herpes virus (EHV). A sign that these experts are thinking along the correct lines is evidence from the racing industry, where little headshaking is seen. This is probably because these mares and their offspring are regularly vaccinated, so foals are not exposed to the virus at this critical age.

Does my horse have a back problem?

If your horse is showing any of the symptoms listed in the panel, he may have a 'back problem'. This can be due to a direct injury to his back, or the result of a problem elsewhere in his body that is causing him to compensate in his back in order to avoid pain.

Muscle injuries

Strenuous physical exertion may cause injury to a horse's muscles and ligaments that will require physiotherapy. Painful muscles contract into a spasm that does not relax and this is often palpable as a hard ridge or knot in the muscle. Careful palpation of the tops of the dorsal spinous processes may suggest that the vertebrae are out of line. In reality, the muscle spasm has pulled the overlying soft tissue to one side, but not the vertebral body

Signs that your horse may have a back problem

There are innumerable signs that your horse may have soreness or muscle spasm in his back. These will vary between individuals, and according to the nature of the problem, the length of time for which it has been present and its severity. Signs to look out for include:

- Sensitivity when being groomed or when manual pressure is applied.
- Stiffness.
- Lameness.
- Change in your horse's movement – holding his head too high, finding collection difficult or becoming short-strided.
- Dislike of being tacked up.
- Change in behaviour or temperament – unexplained bucking, rearing or napping.
- Muscle spasms.
- Headshaking.
- Becoming lethargic.
- Regular shifting of weight.
- Rushing fences.
- Being generally uncomfortable.
- Uneven wear on shoes.

Any changes to normal behaviour, such as unexplained napping, may signal that the horse has a back problem.

General discomfort or resistance to ridden work may be pain-related.

itself. Many physiotherapists and chiropractors are skilled at releasing this muscle spasm and providing relief for the horse. They are not, however, realigning misplaced vertebrae.

Although physical exertion causes back problems, ill-fitting saddles and mild intermittent or undetected bilateral lameness will also give rise to identifiable muscle problems in the back. In order to minimize discomfort or redistribute bodyweight backwards, away from painful front feet for example, the horse may brace his back to accommodate the problem. This commonly results in a spasm in the back muscles. If repeated visits from the physiotherapist are necessary, then veterinary advice may be needed to determine whether a real back problem is present or if the symptoms are secondary to another problem elsewhere.

Poor muscle development over the back or loins can often indicate a chronic underuse or misuse of the hindlimbs. Pain is a common reason and this may arise in any part of the body. Severe muscle wastage, particularly in the neck, will often signal a chronic neck injury or abnormality, and radiography of the neck may be required to identify the problem.

Nerve damage

If there is any significant bony displacement or abnormality, nerve damage or compression may occur. The spinal nerves are branches of the spinal column and exit the bony column through small holes, or foramina, between adjacent vertebrae (see page 19). These nerves control the main muscle mass of the body. Trapping or compression of these nerves will result in impaired muscle function. The end result is that these muscles do not function fully and either develop poorly or even waste.

Detailed investigation

Once lameness has been ruled out as a cause of muscular pain, the back can be investigated in detail. This involves careful palpation of the back muscles to locate areas of spasm, and stimulation of pressure points to make the horse flex his spine to check if a normal range of movement is possible. The most useful clinical evidence can be established by observing the horse in-hand, on the lunge and under saddle. Gait abnormalities are often subtle and require time and patience to identify. The pace that is most affected by back pain is the canter, which also affects the horse's jumping style and enthusiasm.

Further investigation can follow several different routes, and includes:

■ Thermography, which can be employed to identify areas of increased surface heat that in turn may indicate areas of under-lying inflammation.

■ Ultrasonography, an accurate imaging system that will produce an image of the dorsal spinous ligament and locate any tears in the body of the ligament. It can also demonstrate areas where it may be torn from its attachment to the dorsal spinous processes.

■ Radiography, which is very useful because it produces a true picture of the bones themselves as well as the facet joints, the diameter of the spinal canal and any abnormal bone growth.

Wobbler syndrome

Most commonly encountered in large, rapidly growing young horses, this condition is a result of nerve compression. Pinching of the spinal cord due to inadequate ligament support or excess bone growth leads to varying degrees of incoordination and, in extreme cases, the horse being unsteady on his feet.

Back treatments

There is now a good range of treatments available for your horse's back. These should not be thought of as a replacement for conventional veterinary medicine, but rather as a valid complementary treatment. As with any health-related problems or conditions, it is important that your vet is contacted first so that he can assess your horse's condition and investigate any underlying medical conditions that could be causing similar symptoms.

Choosing a specialist

Choose your equine back specialist with care. Your vet may be able to provide a recommendation; alternatively, choose a recognized qualified practitioner.

Osteopathy

Equine osteopathy works on the same principles and theories as human osteopathy, but with specific manipulative techniques modified to take into account the differences between the human and equine bodies.

Osteopathy works primarily through the neuro-muscular system – joints and muscles – and pays special attention to how the internal organs affect and are affected by this system. It is based on the principle that the body is one unit rather than being made up of many parts, with its own self-healing mechanism that can be utilized as part of the treatment.

Consultations normally take around an hour. The practitioner will take a full case history of your horse, including previous veterinary procedures or investigations, the horse's workload and what the problem is. Next, she will touch your horse all over and note any areas of increased temperature or sensitivity. She will also make an assessment of the passive joints, spine and posture. The horse will then be walked and trotted, perhaps on the lunge or ridden, so that his paces can be analysed.

The practitioner will then talk to you about what she has found and produce a course of treatment. This will normally consist of a range of manual techniques designed to suit the individual horse, and may include a stretching programme that also covers specific schooling exercises to complement the treatment. There are no particular guidelines as to how many treatments your horse will need as this depends on the individual.

Physiotherapy

Although physiotherapy can be used to alleviate problems all over the body, it is often used to help treat horses that have back problems, as well as to help improve performance and keep the horse supple and relaxed.

Physiotherapy involves treating problems and maintaining health in your horse's tendons, muscles, ligaments and joints. Sprains and strains can be relieved with physiotherapy and it can help in rehabilitation following orthopaedic surgery. Equine physiotherapists can also help to manage neck, shoulder and pelvic problems.

Physiotherapists use various techniques including manually stretching and massaging parts of the body, using ultrasound, lasers and TENS machines, and prescribing exercise programmes. Treatments vary in length depending on the problem.

Manual treatment is just one of the techniques used by physiotherapists.

Chiropractic

There are numerous common, stressful or traumatic situations – including conformation problems, training and riding equipment, ability of the rider, poor shoeing, direct injury – that can cause abnormal or restricted movement in the spine. Chiropractors call this a 'subluxation', and it may lead to compensatory changes in posture and movement, which in turn cause stress in other joints and muscles.

When treating a horse, a complete chiropractic examination is carried out which is similar to that undertaken by an osteopath or physiotherapist. The chiropractor will perform an adjustment – a very specific, low-force, high-speed, controlled thrust by a hand – on the area of the spine affected, to return the joints to normal movement and relieve any muscle spasms and pain.

The number and frequency of adjustments required to correct a problem depend on the horse's age and condition, the duration of the problem, and its severity. If there is permanent damage, multiple adjustments may be necessary to achieve maximum flexibility, as a return to full movement may not be possible.

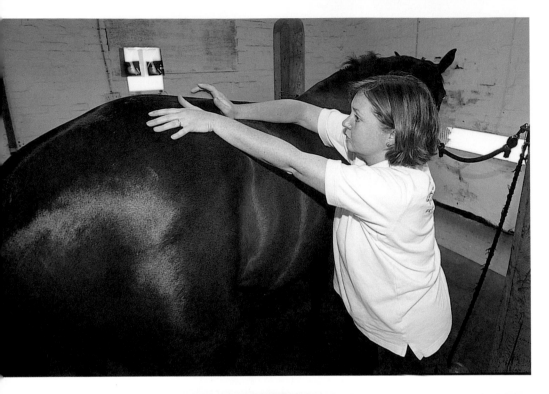

In addition to hands-on treatment from a qualified practitioner, horses with back problems may benefit from 'high-tech' treatments including massage (see page 94), hydrotherapy and solarium sessions.

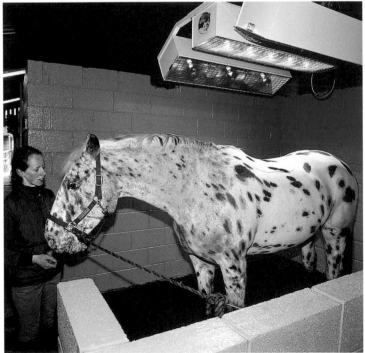

Cold back

Some horses have very sensitive backs and take time to warm up enough to be able to take the weight of the rider: these horses are known as 'cold backed'. Such horses will either round their backs, giving the feeling that they might buck, or lower their backs and sink below the rider. Either way, it is important that the rider keeps a very light seat after mounting. You should hold yourself out of the saddle while the horse walks on and then lower yourself very gently, staying light until he has walked out for a few minutes.

A cold-backed horse should have his back checked by a vet who may, in turn, suggest an equine back specialist. It may be that he is experiencing some discomfort that can be relieved through treatment to release any muscle spasm that is present. The horse may then start to relax and be more confident of

Case study: Remembered pain

I have recently bought a 16.2hh Warmblood. He has suffered back pain in the past due to an ill-fitting saddle, but now has a made-to-measure saddle that fits him well. I have been assured by my vet that he is no longer in pain. However, he sometimes flinches when I go to tack up and occasionally dips his back when I mount, as though he remembers pain. Is this possible?

Even though your vet has assured you that your horse's back is now pain-free, there might possibly still be some low-grade muscle spasm. It would be a good idea also to get a qualified equine physiotherapist to check him over. These people tend to be highly specialized in this area and will also talk to your vet about your horse's situation before they see him – in this way you will have covered every possible cause of pain.

As you rightly suggest, it is likely that your horse's flinching away is related to the memory of his pain, and this is an extremely difficult response to get rid of. However, as long as your horse relaxes and settles once the saddle is on, and you are sure that there are no other problems, he should gradually become more confident that the saddle won't hurt him.

The only other way to break the habit is to spend a few days putting the saddle on, girthing up, then taking it off again. Repeat this process all day until your horse is too bored to respond and/or has become confident that nothing bad or painful is going to happen to him when you saddle up.

stretching through his back. It may help to lunge him for 5–10 minutes before riding to encourage him to stretch and relax. Saddle fit should also be checked.

This sort of problem is not just physical, but also psychological. The horse's fear of his back hurting will persist for a time, even though there is no longer any pain (see Case Study).

Massage aids

There are a number of products on the market that can help owners who feel their horses may benefit from regular massage sessions. These might include horses that are stiff at the start of their work and take some time to warm up, those recovering from back injuries or following therapeutic treatments, and older horses and ponies.

Massage tools range from lightweight, hand-held versions to complete systems of pads plus hand units that would suit a group of owners who wish to club together. Hand-held massagers usually offer variable heads that simulate different massages and help to release tension and muscle cramps, improve muscle tone and circulation, alleviate chronic muscle problems, and aid warming up and cooling down before and after exercise. It is also claimed that they can help tendon and ligament problems, pulled muscles and respiratory difficulties.

The most sophisticated pads are designed to give a deep massage to the whole horse, improve circulation, ease and tone muscles, and promote lymphatic drainage. Some are even effective over the top of rugs.

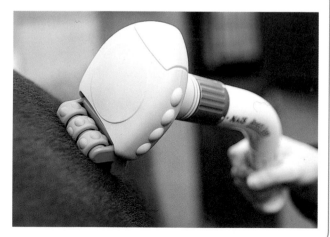

Kissing spines

Kissing spines is a slow, degenerative condition of the bones (spines) that arise from each vertebral bone of the spinal column. These bony processes form the withers and the bony bumps you can feel along a horse's back. When the bones are too close together they compress the soft tissue in between, may tear the fine ligaments that connect adjacent processes, and sometimes even rub together (especially when the horse jumps), when extra bone will develop like a splint and irritate its neighbour, causing pain and inflammation. The problem is usually congenital (the horse was born with it) – for example, the back is abnormally short or curved, so the spines touch during jumping or galloping – but it may have been caused by an injury or accident.

An affected horse will have a sore wither and back area that is swollen and painful to the touch. The condition is confirmed by radiographing the withers and back, which will reveal the abnormal position of the spines. This is important, because kissing spines is sometimes diagnosed when no other cause of back pain can be found.

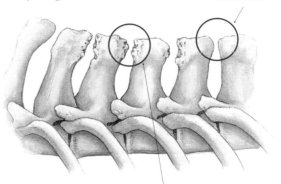

Normal smooth bone surface

Reactive secondary bone growth

Initial treatment is medical and consists of introducing corticosteroids by deep injection into the areas of pain. This can be very effective, allowing the horse to resume normal work. However, it needs to be repeated and its success is governed by the length of time for which your horse responds to this form of treatment.

The surgical option is to remove the spine or spines that are causing the rubbing; however, only alternate spines are removed. Provided the kissing spines are not related to any other condition, the outcome is usually good, with the horse eventually returning to his original workload. Aftercare and recovery time will depend on how the treatment is progressing. As the horse ages, he may be more likely to become stiff in the back due to scarring.

Is my horse lame?

Identifying a lame leg

In trot, a sound horse will hold his head more or less level all the time.

If the horse is lame, he will nod each time his 'good' foreleg lands on the ground, because this leg is taking extra weight. Just to confuse matters, it is possible for a horse to look slightly lame on a foreleg, when in fact the actual problem lies in the diagonal hindleg.

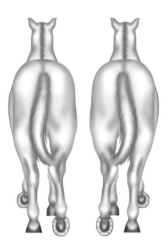

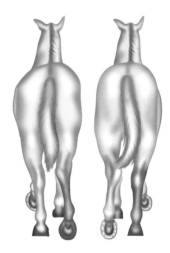

If you watch a sound horse being trotted away from you, you will see that his hips stay level as his hindquarters move. A sound horse will lift both hind feet equally high off the ground, taking an equal amount of weight on each foot as it lands. In addition to this, both hind feet will hit the ground squarely.

If a horse that is lame on a hindleg is trotted away from you, you will see that his hips are uneven as his hindquarters move. The hindquarter on the horse's 'good' side will drop when the sound leg hits the ground because that leg is taking extra weight. Lameness in a foreleg does not usually affect the hindquarters.

Start here

To identify the lame leg, ask a friend to walk or trot your horse in a straight line away from you on a loose rein on level ground. As the horse moves away from you any lameness behind will be obvious. Front leg lameness will show up as he moves towards you. It is important that you see the horse take several strides.

As a general rule, always try to study a lame horse as a whole. For example, look for signs of a fall, such as bleeding on the head. Don't just concentrate on the legs, as the cause of the lameness may be elsewhere.

If any swelling is present on the limbs, reduce by hosing with cold water or using a cold compress (for example, a pack of frozen peas).

Trot the horse on a loose rein to check for lameness.

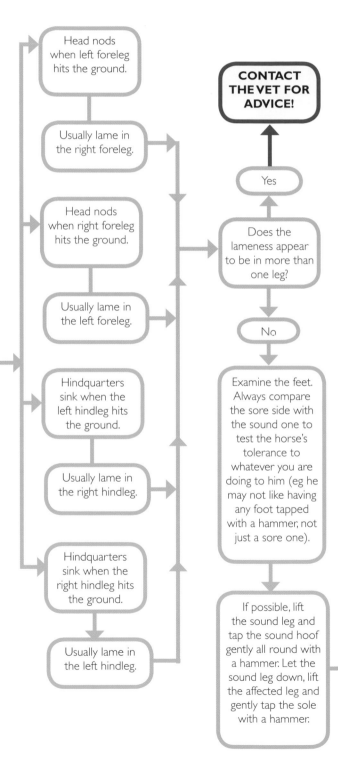

Head nods when left foreleg hits the ground.

Usually lame in the right foreleg.

Head nods when right foreleg hits the ground.

Usually lame in the left foreleg.

Hindquarters sink when the left hindleg hits the ground.

Usually lame in the right hindleg.

Hindquarters sink when the right hindleg hits the ground.

Usually lame in the left hindleg.

Does the lameness appear to be in more than one leg?

Yes → **CONTACT THE VET FOR ADVICE!**

No →

Examine the feet. Always compare the sore side with the sound one to test the horse's tolerance to whatever you are doing to him (eg he may not like having any foot tapped with a hammer, not just a sore one).

If possible, lift the sound leg and tap the sound hoof gently all round with a hammer. Let the sound leg down, lift the affected leg and gently tap the sole with a hammer.

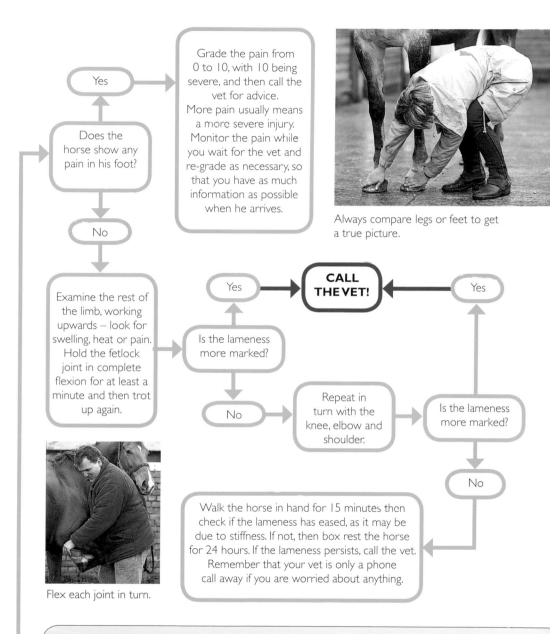

Always compare legs or feet to get a true picture.

Yes → Grade the pain from 0 to 10, with 10 being severe, and then call the vet for advice. More pain usually means a more severe injury. Monitor the pain while you wait for the vet and re-grade as necessary, so that you have as much information as possible when he arrives.

Does the horse show any pain in his foot?

No →

Examine the rest of the limb, working upwards – look for swelling, heat or pain. Hold the fetlock joint in complete flexion for at least a minute and then trot up again.

Is the lameness more marked?

Yes → **CALL THE VET!** ← Yes

No → Repeat in turn with the knee, elbow and shoulder. → Is the lameness more marked?

No →

Walk the horse in hand for 15 minutes then check if the lameness has eased, as it may be due to stiffness. If not, then box rest the horse for 24 hours. If the lameness persists, call the vet. Remember that your vet is only a phone call away if you are worried about anything.

Flex each joint in turn.

Remember:
- The causes of lameness vary greatly, so the information given here is for general guidance only. Always use your common sense when assessing lameness and call your vet for advice if you are at all worried.
- Do not attempt to administer painkillers, for example bute, without seeking veterinary advice.
- It is always better to ring your vet for advice than to treat your horse yourself and make things difficult for the vet at a later stage.

Clinical diagnosis

Lameness is generally an indication of pain in one or more legs. One other type of lameness, mechanical, occurs when there is a stiffness of a joint or contraction of a tendon, causing the horse to move in an abnormal manner. In this type of lameness there is often no pain present.

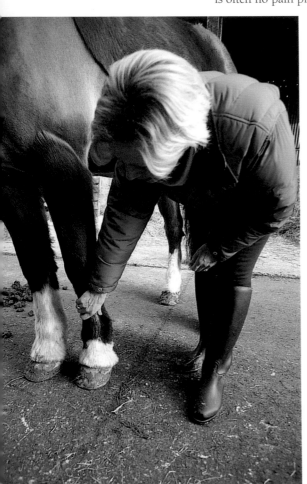

The cause of intermittent lameness can be difficult to pinpoint accurately.

The most common signs of lameness are:

■ The horse rests a foreleg or consistently rests the same hindleg. Often he will point the affected foot forward or hold it off the ground.

■ Severe lameness will be seen even at walk. For less obvious lameness, trotting the horse in hand will reveal the problem area.

If a short period of rest does not completely resolve a lameness, the first stage in any further investigation is to localize the source of pain accurately. To do this, it is necessary to nerve block the leg sequentially, starting at the bottom and working upwards to the point where the lameness resolves. This is essential in every horse, because they cannot tell us where it hurts and we cannot reliably guess.

Sometimes nerve blocks fail to provide the answer we are looking for. In such cases we need to use alternative techniques, such as bone scanning or thermography, and sometimes nuclear magnetic imaging. Unfortunately, these techniques are expensive.

Once the site of the pain has been pinpointed, X-rays can be taken and interpreted with a degree of confidence and accuracy. Once the vet has this information, a diagnosis can be made and a treatment plan formulated that is appropriate and, therefore, likely to succeed.

Intermittent lameness

Sometimes, a horse will suddenly appear lame, as if he has stepped on something sharp, and then go sound again within a few strides. Other horses may be intermittently lame in a less acute fashion.

It can be very frustrating for the attending vet trying to pinpoint the reason for this type of intermittent lameness, because of the lack of consistency in the way the horse moves. The best approach is for the vet to examine the horse's leg thoroughly to see if there are any clues, such as abnormal swellings or pain on palpation. After this has been performed, the vet can assess the horse at walk and trot to see if he can observe any slight lameness, apart from the obvious intermittent attacks.

If this examination localizes a particular area of interest, it can be investigated further by X-ray or ultrasound examination. Occasionally, no clues are found and a horse has to undergo radiography of the entire affected leg. Alternatively, he may be referred to an equine practice that offers scintigraphy – a diagnostic technique used to produce pictures of internal parts of the body.

One of the common reasons for severe intermittent lameness is as simple as a soft-soled horse treading on a stone. A more complicated reason is the presence of a chip of bone in a joint that can cause lameness (see pages 166–167).

Stumbling

Some horses are prone to stumbling and slipping when being ridden, especially on the roads. There are a number of possible causes, including:

- Physical problems in the back or elsewhere.
- Inappropriate trimming and shoeing.
- Lack of fitness.
- Lazy action.
- Poor riding and/or spookiness and lack of concentration in the horse.

Get the horse checked by your vet and, if necessary, a qualified equine back specialist and follow their advice. If after this you suspect your riding may be the problem, take some lessons with a qualified instructor, who will be able to show you how to ride your horse in a way that will help him avoid stumbling in the future.

Laminitis

Laminitis affects thousands of horses and ponies every year. This extremely painful condition occurs when the bond between the dermal and epidermal laminae in the hoof is damaged, causing the pedal bone to become unstable. At worst, the weight of the horse forces the pedal bone to rotate and sink within the foot, sheering arteries and veins and sometimes pushing right through the sole of the foot. If enough of these structures are lost, permanent lameness can result. In this serious situation, in some cases putting the horse or pony to sleep is the kindest option.

While many horses do recover, laminitis often returns. To prevent this happening, your horse needs careful management – and in order to achieve this, you need to understand what causes laminitis, how to prevent it and what to do if your horse gets the disease.

Causes

The actual causes of laminitis are unknown, but there are a number of factors that make an attack more likely.

Obesity The most common factor leading to laminitis. Bacteria in the horse's large intestine ferment excess carbohydrates from either hard feed, lush grass or grass growing under certain conditions, such as stressed or recently frosted. Endotoxins are released when carbohydrate fermentation alters the level of alkalinity, killing bacteria in the large intestine. As with food poisoning, blood is diverted to the gut, leading to a reduced flow to the vessels of the hoof, and potentially to laminitis.

Toxins Bacterial, viral, plant, chemical and fungal toxins have all been linked to the onset of laminitis. Before an improvement can be seen in the horse's condition, these toxins must be removed through effective treatment.

Trauma to the hoof Constant hammering on hard surfaces can damage the laminae and increase the likelihood of laminitis.

Mechanical Incorrect shoeing that puts pressure on the hoof sole, allowing the hoof to grow too long, can lead to laminitis.

Drugs Giving a stressed or susceptible horse corticosteroids – drugs produced from adrenal hormones – may cause laminitis. Administering corticosteroids to overweight ponies suffering from sweet itch can be particularly dangerous.

Cushing's disease Tumours on the pituitary gland cause Cushing's disease and laminitis tends to go hand-in-hand with this condition. Signs that a horse is suffering from Cushing's include a curly coat that doesn't moult, increased drinking and puffy pads above the eyes.

Stress A horse that is prone to stress can suffer from laminitis, although this is rare. Overworking an unfit horse, travelling

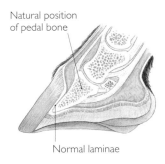

Natural position of pedal bone

Normal laminae

Normal hoof

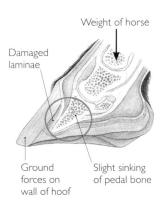

Weight of horse

Damaged laminae

Ground forces on wall of hoof

Slight sinking of pedal bone

Laminitic hoof

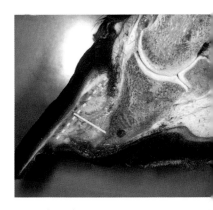

In this foot, the attachment between the pedal bone and hoof wall has failed.

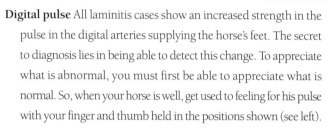
him for long periods or even giving a vaccination can all add to a horse's stress levels.

Other triggers Cold weather and the onset of oestrus in mares can occasionally cause an attack of laminitis in vulnerable horses.

Symptoms

Feel your horse's pulse with your finger and thumb held in the positions shown.

Digital pulse All laminitis cases show an increased strength in the pulse in the digital arteries supplying the horse's feet. The secret to diagnosis lies in being able to detect this change. To appreciate what is abnormal, you must first be able to appreciate what is normal. So, when your horse is well, get used to feeling for his pulse with your finger and thumb held in the positions shown (see left).

When your horse has laminitis the pulse rate will increase and, importantly, the character of the pulse will also change. In a normal horse the pulse should feel as if it has a gradual rise, peak and then fall at about 40 beats per minute. When a horse has laminitis there is a rapid peak to the pulse and the pulse is much stronger (easier to feel). It becomes like a tiny hammer under your finger and thumb.

Lameness This is the other defining characteristic of laminitis. In mild cases, the horse will not be able to walk as freely as usual and will tend to shift his weight constantly from one foot to another, trying to stand on his heels. Remember that he may get laminitis in any combination of feet, with the front feet most commonly affected.

Heat Feeling for heat in the feet is very inconsistent and should not be used to diagnose laminitis.

Hoof depression If the laminitis has progressed to acute founder, there is a depression present around the front part of the coronary band. This is because the laminae at the front of the foot have separated and the pedal bone has dropped within the hoof capsule. As it does so it pulls the skin down with it, creating the depression you can feel with your finger.

If the laminitis has progressed to the stage of a sinker, the depression extends all the way around the coronary band,

right back to both heels, since all the laminae have separated. Sinkers do not adopt the heel loading stance associated with laminitis; instead, they are very reluctant to move and often slap down their feet as they are no longer properly attached to their hooves.

The typical stance of a laminitic horse is with the weight borne on the heels, hindlegs well under and forefeet stretched out in front.

Vital signs In severe cases the horse may be sweaty with quickened breathing. Rectal temperature and heart (pulse) rate may be raised.

Founder and sinker

In first-time laminitis cases displacement of the pedal bone in relation to the hoof capsule depends on the severity of the inflammation. Laminitis is caused by the redistribution of blood flow away from the sensitive laminae, starving them of nutrients and

A depression at the front of the coronary band indicates acute founder.

In the case of a sinker, the depression can be felt right back to the heels.

 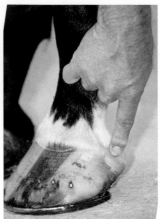

oxygen. If this shortage of blood flow is extensive or prolonged, then the horse is likely to deteriorate to the stage of acute founder. This begins when the weight of the pony starts to overcome the cohesion between the laminae and the hoof capsule in his feet. The front part of his hooves begins to separate, just like a fingernail being pulled off from the quick beneath.

Whether an affected pony will recover depends on whether the cause is treatable and how much pedal bone displacement has occurred in his feet. A vet can evaluate this from marked X-rays, measuring the vertical distance through which the pedal bone has dropped in relation to the top of the front hoof wall (the founder distance). This is the most reliable radiological prognostic indicator for acute founder cases.

If a horse or pony recovers, his feet will be deformed. The hooves will show growth rings on the walls that are more widely spaced at the heels than the toe (see left). The soles will not be as concave as before and the white line around the toe will be wider than normal. This stretched white line can no longer protect the foot from bacterial infections, which is why seedy toe is a common consequence of founder cases. If the feet are not correctly trimmed on a regular basis (every five weeks) they will become overlong in the toes and the heels will grow higher than normal.

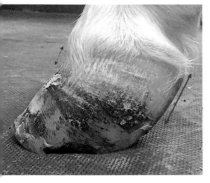

Chronic laminitis will result in deformed hooves.

Horses or ponies with sinker have lost all laminar attachment, so the pedal bone moves straight down within the hoof capsule.

Sinkers often shed the hoof capsule as a whole and only 20% of sinker cases survive. Survivors do not develop the distorted foot characteristic of recovered acute founder cases; they grow a normal-looking foot with one deep growth ring around the wall. This grows out over a period of about nine months.

Emergency action

If your horse does get laminitis, follow this emergency plan:

1 Always call your vet at the first suspicion of laminitis, as quick action can sometimes make all the difference to the progress of the disease. He may fit your horse with frog supports if you have not already done so (see panel)

2 Do not feed your horse until the vet has been to assess him.

3 Remove the horse from grass.

4 Stable him. If you are a long way from the stable, transport him in a trailer.

5 Provide him with a good bed, preferably shavings, at least 45cm (18in) deep.

6 Keep him relaxed and encourage him to lie down.

7 Keep him stabled for 30 days after he is sound without the use of painkillers.

Give some support

Frog supports are an essential addition to your first-aid kit if your horse is prone to laminitis. Made from a high-performance foam that does not lose its spring, they provide invaluable support to the laminae that form a bond between the pedal bone and hoof wall, and are simply bandaged into place.

Feeding a laminitic horse

The only way to help prevent laminitis nutritionally is to restrict your horse's access to rich pasture and feed a balanced high-fibre diet that is low in sugar, starch and fructans.

The link between sugar in grass and laminitis

It is perfectly acceptable for horses to eat sugar – they have evolved over thousands of years to be able to seek out the sweetest grass. But, just like us, they can suffer if they eat too much.

Sugars found in grasses are easily digested and absorbed by the horse. However, plants store sugars as a future energy source in the form of fructans, and these are not as easily digested as the sugar. Enzymes in the small intestine cannot break down

Feeding carbohydrate-filled cereals could trigger laminitis.

Prevention is better than cure

- Try not to let your horse get fatter than a condition score of 3 (see pages 110–115). Limit the amount of grass to which he has access by fitting him with a muzzle or fencing off a smaller area of his field and strip grazing it. Alternatively, you could allow your horse out to grass for a limited period only, with the remainder of his time spent in a dieting paddock, arena or barn.
- Make sure you give your horse only the necessary concentrates in his hard feed and select these carefully (see right).
- Avoid prolonged or fast trotting on the roads. Also, be aware of ground conditions for fast work and at competitions, especially in the summer. Traumatic laminitis is not uncommon in jumping ponies.
- Try to avoid stressing your horse any more than is strictly necessary.

fructans, resulting in starch overload in the hindgut. Rapidly fermenting starch in the hindgut is the trigger factor for diseases such as laminitis and colic.

Fructans levels in the grass vary depending on the weather and the time of day. For example, if the day is dull and overcast then the plant will be producing little sugar so little fructans will accumulate. But on a cold, frosty day the plant hangs on to the fructans so levels will be high. It may be safer to graze a laminitis-prone horse from 11pm to 6am, when levels of fructans are generally lower.

Low-sugar options

It is a big mistake to try to limit the amount of forage in your horse's diet in a bid to reduce his sugar consumption, as forage is the most important part of his diet. If you need to limit your horse's grass intake because he is prone to laminitis, low-sugar forage options include:

- Oat or barley straw (can be mixed with hay in a haynet).
- Short chop feeds. These are basically chaff (chopped forage) that has been cut into short pieces. They can be fed as a forage alternative or mixed with hard feed.
- Late-cut, mature meadow hay.

If you need to feed your horse concentrates, choose a low-energy feed that is high in fibre and low in sugar. Cereal feeds should be avoided as they contain a lot of sugar which is stored in the form of starch, so instead feed a low-sugar chop with a vitamin and mineral supplement or feed balancer added. Sugars can't really be hidden in manufactured hard feeds as everything has to be listed on the bag.

Caring for laminitic hooves

Laminitis damages the laminae that hold the hoof on to the pedal bone. They support the horse's weight when normal, but when diseased they have a huge burden placed upon them.

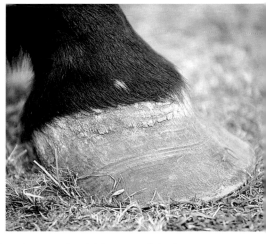

The laminae form part of the white line – the line between the wall and sole of the hoof – as they eventually grow down the foot. Therefore, damaged laminae lead to a less-than-ideal white line. Also, laminitic horses tend to grow long toes, leading to a hoof conformation described as slipper toe. This stretches the white line, further compromising it. Thirdly, the damage to the laminae produces dead lamina tissue at various sites. If this tissue is small enough, the body may be able to reabsorb it, but if there is too much it can form a sterile abscess which is similar to a normal foot abscess (see page 172).

The resolution of the problem lies in regular foot trimming to keep the toe short and rolled, special attention to picking out the feet and good hygiene. The use of hydrogen peroxide or formalin washes on a regular basis will help to keep the hooves clean as well as making them tougher (ask your vet for advice).

Laminitis can result in foot abnormalities and problems such as seedy toe that take time and care to resolve.

Ordinary shoes may not be the best thing if your horse's hooves have sunk or rotated and the pedal bone has changed its position within the hoof capsule. Special laminitic shoes are available that can be glued or nailed on. These support the sole, raise the heels and keep the toe short and rolled to bring the break-over point as far back as possible. All these measures will help the horse back towards soundness.

Controlling your horse's weight

Excessive energy intake, leading to obesity, may now be the number one danger facing most leisure horses. Monitoring your horse's bodyweight is an effective means of tracking energy balance, but to get a truly accurate representation of energy status, you should know his body fat composition.

Condition scoring is a practical way to monitor body fat content, and it can be quite accurate when done correctly. Keeping track of your horse's weight and condition can help you to identify potential health issues before they become a problem.

Mature horses

Often, changes of condition in horses do not become noticeable to the eye until it is too late, which is why keeping regular records of your horse's weight and condition is so important. This allows you to adjust feeding programmes accordingly, before you have a problem on your hands. Overweight horses and ponies are more prone to colic and, of course, laminitis.

It is easy to blame equine obesity on greediness. However, human influence is an important factor. Some of us are guilty of 'plumping up' horses to 'show condition'. A bodyweight that looks ideal to you, and perhaps some judges, may not be physiologically ideal for your horse.

Growing horses

Weekly monitoring of a growing horse's weight and condition can help to identify whether he is at risk of developmental problems that are the result of growth plates (see pages 13 and 17) failing under the added strain of the weanling or yearling that is gaining too much weight. You may need to reduce his feed intake, and a veterinary surgeon and nutritionist should be consulted. Do not worry that reducing feed will compromise your horse's eventual size – it is difficult to slow down a horse's skeletal growth. However, it is important to monitor his growth curve in order to control rapid gains in fat.

Condition scoring

Condition scoring was developed to help eliminate some of the inaccuracies of bodyweight calculations and is a visual assessment of your horse using descriptions of fatness or thinness.

Calculating your horse's weight

Many surveys have shown that owners routinely underestimate or overestimate their horses' bodyweight, and this includes experienced horsemen. One study found that only 12% of horsemen used scales to weigh their horses, 53% used a weightape and 68% said they simply guessed their horses' weights.

Scales The most accurate method of calculating your horse's weight is to use scales. Unfortunately, few of us have the luxury of owning such equipment. However, it is well worth loading your horse into a lorry and taking him to a local weighbridge, or perhaps using the scales at your veterinary surgery. Having an accurate record of your horse's weight is a useful basis against which you can compare subsequent weightape measurements.

continued overleaf

continued

Weightapes These offer a simple and practical solution. They are about 90% accurate, provided that the horse is standing square and on a level surface. His head should be in a normal position and he should be relaxed. The tape should be dropped over the lowest part of the withers and should pass underneath him as close to his front legs as possible. It should naturally follow a slightly angled line. The tape should be firm but not so tight that it causes an indent in the horse's flesh. The height of the horse is also an important variable. Weightapes that are calibrated to take this into account provide an improved estimate of equine bodyweight.

Areas of particular interest in condition scoring

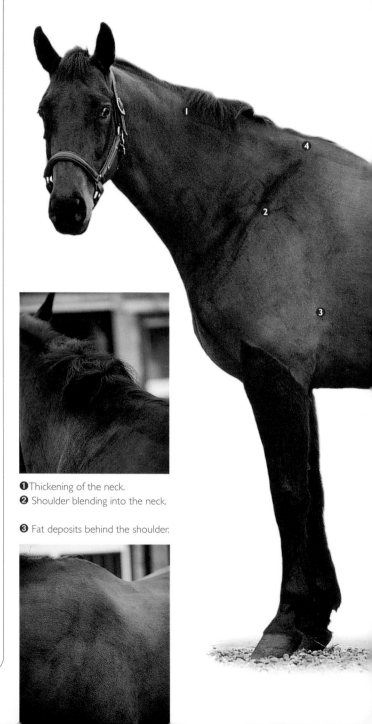

❶ Thickening of the neck.
❷ Shoulder blending into the neck.

❸ Fat deposits behind the shoulder.

❹ Fat covering along the withers.

❺ Coverage on the backbone.

❻ Fat covering on the hips and on the buttock area.

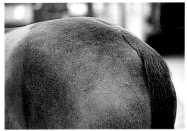

❼ Fat deposits around the tailhead.
❽ Fat deposits around the sheath and udder.

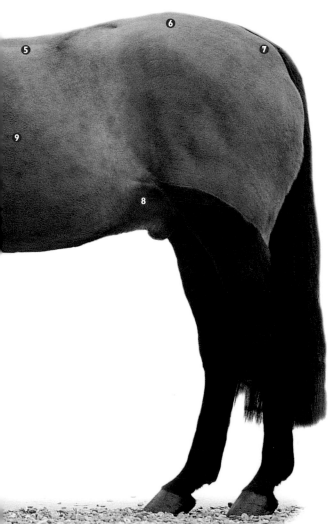

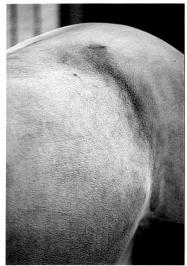

❾ Fat covering the ribs.

Condition score 4.5 (fat/very fat).

Condition score 1 (poor).

As well as a visual assessment, you also use touch to assess the body fat covering particular points of the horse's skeleton, which can be graded on a scale of 0–5 (or sometimes 1–9).

A combination of girth measurement and body condition score is the most accurate alternative to weighing with scales. It may take time and practice to develop a systematic approach that you can reproduce accurately on a daily basis.

When you are seeking feeding advice or calculating your horse's nutritional requirements, simply knowing your horse's weight is not enough and body condition scoring should become part of your routine. Familiarizing yourself with condition scoring will increase your accuracy in weight determination and reap benefits for your horse husbandry.

If your horse takes in more energy as food than he uses up in exercise, temperature control and metabolism, he will get fat. If he takes in less energy than he needs, he will lose weight. Native breeds, cobs and some warmbloods have efficient metabolisms and are more likely to put on weight, while Thoroughbred types have a tendency to lose weight easily.

Condition	Neck and shoulder	Withers	Back and loins	Hindquarters	Ribs
0 Very poor	Bone structure can be felt easily, no muscle shelf where neck meets shoulder	Bone structure can be felt easily	Three points of vertebrae can be felt easily	Tailhead and hipbones projecting	Each rib can be felt easily
1 Poor (eg some older horses with very poor dentition etc)	Bone structure can be felt, slight shelf where neck meets shoulder	Bone structure can be felt	Spinous processes can be felt easily, transverse processes have slight fat covering	Hipbones can be felt	Slight fat covering but ribs can still be felt
2 Moderate (eg mares milking towards the end of the grass season)	Fat covering over bone structure	Fat deposits over withers	Dependent upon conformation	Fat covering over hipbones	Fat covering over spinous processes. Ribs not visible but can still be felt
3 Good (eg show condition)	Neck flows smoothly into shoulder	Neck rounds out of withers	Back is level	Hipbones cannot be felt	Layer of fat over ribs
4 Fat (good doer and increasing risk of laminitis)	Fat deposits along neck	Fat padded around withers	Positive crease along back	Hipbones cannot be felt	Fat spongy over and between ribs
5 Very fat	Bulging fat	Bulging fat	Deep, positive crease	Pockets of fat	Pockets of fat

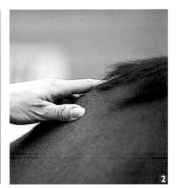

1 Feel along the top of your horse's neck and down to the point where the neck joins the shoulder.
2 Run your hands down both sides of the withers.
3 Continue along the back, feeling for the spinous processes or fat on either side of the backbone.
4 Feel the hindquarters and tailhead for projecting bones or fat deposits.
5 Press firmly around the ribcage to assess the fat coverage over the ribs.

How to do it

The first step in condition scoring involves taking the time to stand back and observe your horse critically. The second step involves actually feeling your horse with your hands. This does not mean simply running your hands over his ribs. With practice, some light prodding will enable you to tell the crucial difference between muscle and fat.

The table opposite shows you how to assign a condition score to your horse. The horse in the photograph on pages 112–113 has a condition score of 3.5. Ideally, you should be aiming to achieve a condition score of between 2.5 and 3. Horses with this score are less at risk of serious, life-threatening conditions such as laminitis.

There may be situations where a horse's condition will fall between scores and you may need to assign a half score. For example, a score of 2.5 would be a fit horse in competition or an endurance horse.

Other factors

When you are condition scoring, remember that factors such as a long, thick coat and some conformational differences can make it difficult to apply certain criteria to a specific animal. Horses with prominent withers, those who are flat across the back and heavily in-foal mares (the weight of the foal pulls the skin tight over the ribs) may have a body condition score that appears lower than it really is.

Azoturia

These days, most vets refer to azoturia, and its milder form 'tying up', as equine rhabdomyolysis syndrome (ERS) or exertional rhabdomyolysis. Rhabdomyolysis literally means inflammation of the muscles. Other terms used are exertional myopathy (myopathy means muscle cell damage) and recurrent exertional rhabdomyolysis.

Unfortunately, ERS can affect any horse, whatever his type, breed, age or sex, so it is wise to be alert to the problem. The condition affects horses' muscles so that they cannot function normally, leading to a partial or complete inability to move.

This results in a wide range of possible clinical signs. A show pony, for instance, may fail to lengthen when asked, or a racehorse could start to slow in the closing stages of a race. Most typical, though, is the horse that is suddenly unable or unwilling to move. Sometimes a horse will actually go down and be unable to get back up. These stiff or immobile horses are the easiest to recognize as potential sufferers.

Signs tend to become obvious during exercise, but not always at the start, and will vary between individuals and even the same horse suffering different attacks. Once a horse has had a bout he may well be susceptible to future problems, although the time period between them can vary widely from days to months. The initial return to work is one of the most common times for a repeat episode.

Symptoms of ERS vary, but a racehorse, for example, may start to slow towards the end of a race.

What happens during an attack?

During an episode the affected horse will often be in some pain and distress, although this tends to vary with the individual and the extent of the damage. Usually it is the muscles of the hindlimbs that are most severely affected, but in a few horses the forelimbs can also be involved. Muscles may be swollen and/or painful to the touch, but this is not always the case, especially if the condition is mild. The affected area is normally quite generalized over one or more muscle groups, compared with the more localized pain that is typical of pulled or strained muscles.

Causes

We now believe this condition is caused by a number of factors, and it can even occur in horses that have not been heavily exercised. These days, it is rare for horses to die from the condition, but there are perhaps more cases of the milder forms than in the past. In particular, we are increasingly seeing the problem in horses that are regularly exercised with perhaps no immediately obvious reason for the episode. This could reflect our increased awareness of the problem, or it could be to do with the way we manage and feed our horses today.

Most sufferers seem to have an underlying susceptibility, which may then be triggered by one or more contributory factors, usually including exercise. Reasons for an underlying susceptibility could include metabolic, biochemical, hormonal, nutritional or circulatory abnormalities, while contributory factors could include temperament and management, especially feeding. Other circumstances to take into account include the possibility of an infection and even the weather.

Because there are so many varied causes of the condition, it is not always possible to recommend specific management routines that may help each and every sufferer – what works for one individual may not work for another.

Recurrent exertional rhabdomyolysis

This is due to an abnormality in the process of muscle contraction. It is found mainly in Thoroughbreds, Standardbreds and Arabs, especially in the young, nervous filly in racing training. Affected animals often have frequent attacks, with persistent levels in the blood of a marker (aspartate aminotransferase) that indicates soft tissue and muscle damage.

Trigger factors appear to be training at a gallop but restraining the horse from reaching top speeds, prolonged periods of box rest, high-grain diets, excitement and the presence of a concurrent lameness. It may be an inherited condition. Confirmation of the diagnosis involves muscle biopsies and intensive laboratory tests, and therefore is rarely undertaken.

Some Arab horses can be prone to recurrent exertional rhabdomyolysis.

Polysaccharide storage myopathy (PSSM)

This is caused by a defect in the way glucose is handled and stored in the muscles, and mostly affects the hindlimbs. Affected animals have high levels of a normal (glycogen) as well as an abnormal (polysaccharide) storage form of glucose in their muscle. PSSM is found mainly in Quarter Horses and related breeds such as some Arabs, Standardbreds and Thoroughbreds. In these breeds there appears to be an hereditary basis. Draught horses and Warmbloods appear to suffer from a related condition with slightly modified clinical signs.

In the USA, detailed research has been conducted into a condition essentially the same as PSSM, but known as Equine Polysaccharide Storage Myopathy (EPSM), in draught horses, in which it appears to be particularly common, severe and hard-to-diagnose. In these horses, it has been identified as a cause of severe muscle wasting and weakness, tying up, poor performance, shivers and other abnormal hindlimb movement and, most devastating of all, inability to rise due to weakness during work, foaling, at rest or following general anaesthesia. At the present time, diagnosis is best made by examining a muscle biopsy for the characteristic changes.

Horses with this disease seem not to be able to derive adequate muscle energy from carbohydrates, which are the main source of energy in grains, sweet feeds and pelleted horse feeds. Carbohydrates are also a major source of energy in hay and pasture, but dietary treatment does not affect these: it involves decreasing the amount of other carbohydrates and replacing them with fat as an energy source (pages 122–123). To date, this dietary therapy appears to be extremely effective, with many cases showing 100% improvement, but is most effective when it is started in earlier stages of the disease. PSSM may very well prove to be a disease that is more easily prevented than treated.

Trigger factors include being rested for a few days prior to exercise, infection and, most importantly, diet. Affected horses tend to have calmer temperaments than the other subgroup, and often have persistent levels in the blood of an enzyme (creatine kinase) indicating muscle damage, without clinical signs necessarily being present. PSSM may have a higher incidence than previously thought. On biopsy, the muscle fibres contain large amounts of the abnormal polysaccharide.

Diagnosis

If your horse has just suffered an episode of ERS, it is important to realize that it could have been triggered by a combination of unfortunate one-off factors that may never happen again. Hopefully, once back in work your horse will not suffer another episode in his life.

Unfortunately, some horses are not so lucky and seem to suffer from recurrences of this condition on a regular basis. However, one should not assume that a horse that has had one full confirmed episode is having another attack every time he goes a bit stiff.

The provisional diagnosis of ERS is usually based on the horse's clinical history, plus his current signs, and is then confirmed by monitoring plasma muscle enzyme activities as well as (in PSSM) by means of a muscle biopsy. Because the clinical signs can be so variable, the condition can be relatively easy or difficult to diagnose.

Treatment

Veterinary treatment is not always necessary – it depends on how severely the horse is affected – but you should always call your vet if you suspect an attack of ERS. Depending on the individual case, treatment may aim to limit further muscle damage, decrease any pain and anxiety, restore fluid balance and maximize the chance of a speedy return to work.

Monitoring before and during the return to work, by means of blood tests, can be valuable, especially for a horse that suffers repeat episodes. Samples will need to be taken before and then two to six hours after appropriate exercise, to check for enzymes that indicate muscle damage.

Preventing further attacks

Unfortunately, there is no single step or set of procedures that can guarantee to prevent further episodes – but appropriate management (see panel on page 124) and feeding may help. It can be a good idea to keep a record of events for horses that suffer repeat episodes.

The diet that is best for a horse that may be susceptible to ERS or is recovering from an episode depends on the individual animal, his workload and type, as well as the history of his attacks. But there are some general principles you can follow.

Taking 10–15 minutes to warm up and cool down at walk can help to prevent tying up.

Feeding forage

If your horse's energy needs can be met by forage alone, then this is likely to be the best way forward. Check that he is maintaining a good bodyweight and consider whether he is giving you the sort of ride you want.

Most of your horse's diet should be forage.

- If you are feeding forage alone, you will need to provide a vitamin and mineral supplement to make up for any deficiencies in such a diet.
- For most horses, it is best not to feed large quantities of alfalfa or other legume-rich hays. However, small amounts of alfalfa chaff can be helpful for horses in hard work. The chaff should be fed in increasing amounts in conjunction with any increasing workload.
- Other fibre sources can be fed in addition to straight forage. Good alternatives, especially for horses who may need more energy than forage alone can provide, include unmolassed, soaked sugarbeet pulp, appropriately prepared, and soya hulls. High-fibre feeds that contain highly digestible fibre sources are now available.
- Finally, avoid turning your horse out on to lush, fast-growing pastures, although prolonged turnout in a sparse paddock is often helpful.

Additional complementary feeding

If your horse needs more energy than he can get from forage alone, you will need to look at suitable complementary concentrate feeds or supplementing with oil (see opposite). You can often get help from feed companies, who will arrange for a nutritionist to analyse your horse's diet.

- Choose a fibre-based, low-starch feed, especially one low in oats. Ideally, this should be fed at the manufacturer's recommended level. However, if you need to feed more to maintain condition or to get the type of ride you want, consider adding some supplementary oil instead of extra concentrate feed.
- If you do not have to feed as much as the recommended level, change to an even lower-energy feed or add an appropriate

amount of a suitable vitamin and mineral supplement (contact the manufacturer's helpline for advice).

- Do not add wheat bran to your horse's diet as this can give an unbalanced calcium-to-phosphorus ratio.
- Horses suffering from PSSM should not be fed any cereal starch and their sugar intake should be kept as low as possible.
- Do not feed more because you expect your horse's workload to increase – wait until it has.

Feeding oil

Alternatively, consider supplementing with oil, which can avoid some of the problems of feeding starch. If a manufactured high-oil feed is used, it must be high-oil, low-starch and preferably high-fibre.

Take care when adding concentrates to your horse's diet – choose a fibre-based, low-starch feed.

The other option is vegetable oils, such as corn oil or soya oil – preferably human grade. Choose the one that is most palatable and digestible for your horse. Do not give animal fats as they can cause digestive upsets and are often unpalatable. If you add oil to your horse's diet, do it slowly and be aware that it has the potential to create multiple imbalances – get expert advice if you are in any doubt.

Oil doesn't provide any additional protein, minerals or, often, vitamins (the vitamin E content is variable), so you will need to give an additional vitamin and mineral supplement.

Seek advice from your vet as regards types and quantities for all these supplements.

Selenium and vitamin E

These are important antioxidant nutrients for all horses, whether or not they suffer from ERS. It is unlikely that vitamin E/selenium deficiency is the primary cause in most cases of the syndrome but, in certain individuals, deficiency may be a contributing factor. Again, seek advice from your vet.

Salt and minerals

Appropriate electrolyte (calcium, magnesium, sodium and potassium) supplementation can reduce the frequency of episodes or

Tips for managing a horse with tying up

Initially

- Avoid forced walking: get your vet to treat the horse where he suffered the episode.
- In severe cases, where transport is needed, a lorry is preferable to a trailer (as long as the ramp is not too steep) as horses tend to expend less muscular effort travelling in a lorry than a trailer. Whatever the transport used, ideally the horse should be safely supported in such a way that further muscular effort is kept to a minimum.
- Put your horse in a clean, dry stable (so that you can tell that urination has occurred), away from draughts.
- Provide grass hay and, if necessary later on, a small meal of a high-fibre pellet – which can be soaked so that it forms a moist gruel.

Proceed to the next stage when

- Your horse has been moving freely around the stable for several hours.
- There are no signs of pain when the muscles are felt and the horse does not resent this palpation any more than usual.
- The urine is not discoloured by myoglobin – a reddish-brown pigmenting protein released from damaged muscle. If in doubt over when to proceed, contact your vet.

When able to proceed

- Turn out into a small field or indoor school (rather than start in-hand or ridden exercise), but avoid lush pastures or letting your horse get cold.
- Encourage gentle movement in the field (eg turn out with a quiet known companion, put any forage/feed and water at opposite ends of the area).
- If your horse is excitable, it may be worth discussing this first with your vet.

Starting to ride again

- In mild cases, you may be able to start riding after just two or three days in the field, unless directed otherwise by your vet. In more severe or repeat cases, wait until the muscle enzyme activities have returned to within acceptable limits (your vet will advise on this).
- Especially in the initial stages of a return to work, avoid lungeing, horse walkers, work in tight circles and hill work.
- Implement strict 10- to 15-minute warm-up and cool-down periods at walk only. This is to allow for adequate blood flow to the muscles before and after asking your horse to perform.
- Slowly increase the intensity and duration of the exercise and, if your horse misbehaves on his own or in company, ride alone or with others as appropriate.
- Daily exercise or turnout often seems to be valuable – but continue to avoid turning out your horse on lush pastures.
- Decrease the workload and concentrate feed if there is any suspicion of a respiratory viral infection on the yard.

When in work again

- Stick to regular daily exercise.
- Avoid the use of horse walkers.
- If daily exercise is not possible, turn out for as long as you can on rest days. Reduce any supplementary feed intake by half from the evening before the day of rest until the evening after.
- If your horse is to have a prolonged period of rest, re-evaluate his diet so that you are feeding a lower energy content or pure forage (which should be supplemented with vitamins and minerals).

prevent further episodes in a number of recurrent sufferers. It is, therefore, important to ensure that your horse's diet provides enough of these electrolytes in a balanced manner. If in doubt, check with the feed manufacturer.

In recurrent cases, it may be worth your vet checking out your horse's individual need for electrolytes through blood and urine analysis.

Note the following points:

- Salt should be provided for all horses.
- For horses in little or no work, providing a salt block may be adequate (but ensure that it is sited so that its use by an affected horse can be monitored).
- Where complementary feed or a vitamin and mineral supplement is being fed, any block should be a pure salt rather than a mineralized one.
- Do not use salt blocks made for other animals.
- For horses in more work, or who sweat noticeably, you may need to add salt to the feed. Ask your vet about suitable quantities for your horse.

Ride out in company if it helps to keep your horse calm.

Shivers

Shivers is a neurological condition that affects the horse's hind-limbs, and occasionally the front limbs. In mild cases, it creates a very slight tremor in a hindleg when it is lifted off the ground. The tail may also be raised and shiver, and the neck may be extended. Shiverers rarely have difficulty going forward, but the condition becomes worse if the horse is made to walk backwards, when it is difficult for him to pick up his hindlegs. This consequently makes shoeing very difficult. In severe cases, there is continuous trembling of the hindlegs and weakness of the hindquarters in general.

The condition slowly becomes worse and can lead to more general lack of co-ordination, especially at walk. Mild cases can progress to severe cases over variable periods of time, usually measured in months or years.

The cause of this disease is not clearly under-stood. It usually becomes worse with age and there is no known treatment to alleviate the symptoms or treat the cause. It does not usually get so bad that euthanasia is necessary, but is obviously worrying for both horse and owner. If your horse is suffering from this condition, you must gauge carefully when it is no longer safe to ride him.

Shivers is a neurological condition affecting the horse's hindlimbs. The symptoms are the result of an imbalance between the action of the flexor and extensor muscles, which cause a spasm that is slow to relax.

Stringhalt

Stringhalt is a condition characterized by a sharp, involuntary flexing of the hock joint of either hindleg. The cause of the problem is unknown. The condition can be treated by surgery, involving the removal of the lateral digital extensor tendon. The outlook after surgery can be variable, but many horses do show an improvement.

If the signs of the problem are mild, such as simply stamping a hind foot on the ground, the horse can continue in work, with surgery becoming an option only if the condition worsens.

Arthritis

Arthritis is inflammation in a joint or the degeneration of its function. It tends to affect older horses and is generally caused by general wear and tear on their joints and the thinning of joint cartilage. Degenerative joint disease (DJD) is a general term used to describe arthritis that is degenerative and progressive. Specific conditions like navicular and spavin are also forms of DJD.

Joint anatomy

Joints are constructed in many forms and can range from a simple hinge joint, such as the fetlock, to a ball-and-socket joint, like the hip. Most simple joints involve two bones articulating (forming a joint) with each other where they meet. Some joints, like the knee and hock, are constructed with many bones, each articulating with its neighbour. The overall effect is that the full range of movement is greater than that achieved by a simple joint.

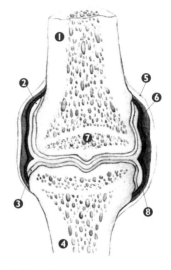

Joint anatomy

❶ Bone
❷ Synovial fluid
❸ Articular cartilage
❹ Bone
❺ Ligament
❻ Joint capsule
❼ Subchondral bone
❽ Synovial membrane

What goes wrong?

Any joint structure can be injured, usually by physical trauma associated with excessive use or overbending. In such a case, a joint may have been forced through a greater-than-normal range of movement, thus straining the joint structures.

Hard ground creates further problems for horses. Under these conditions the joints must absorb all the concussion by flexion, because the ground has no give – ultimately, this leads to inflamed joints. In such cases it is easy for the joint capsule and ligaments to become stretched or even torn, which may result in the synovial membranes going into overdrive and producing excess fluid. Because the capsule is stretched, fluid is produced until all the elasticity is taken up and the back-pressure can limit the volume. There is now a balance between production and resorption of fluid; the capsule will remain enlarged until it begins to contract as the inflammation in the capsule repairs. If the capsule does not reduce to its original size, because the trauma was too severe or was repeated too often, you are left with a permanently enlarged joint capsule even after the inflammation has repaired.

Good examples of this are articular windgalls in a fetlock (see page 158). Such changes are the early stages of arthritis, but the good news is that they may not lead to lameness if the initial signs of joint swelling are recognized and enough time is allowed for the joint to settle before strenuous work is recommenced. This early warning sign of arthritis is more accurately referred to as synovitis – inflammation of the synovial membrane.

True arthritis

Extreme or repeated trauma can cause more severe damage to the articular cartilage, causing it to tear or bruise. This leaves grooves known as wear lines. In some cases, these areas of defect may be ulcer-like. In the worst cases, the loss of cartilage may be so severe that the underlying subchondral bone is exposed. Such lesions are very painful because the nerve endings in the bone are exposed, having lost their protective layer of cartilage. Now we are entering the realms of true arthritis.

The symptoms vary from slight stiffness to obvious lameness. There may also be swelling, heat and pain when the area is flexed. Normally symptoms are worse during cold, wet spells or if the horse is kept stabled for long periods of time.

Complex joints, such as the knee and hock, are prone to excess bone production where cartilage loss has occurred. This is usually on the outer margins of the bones and is easily visible on X-rays. Changes involving only cartilage loss cannot usually be seen radiographically.

Bone spavin

One exception to this occurs in the hock, where loss of joint space can be seen on an X-ray. This loss is caused by degeneration of the cartilage, plus new bone formation invading the joint space. The end result is that two adjacent bones become fused together with total loss of the joint. This condition is known as

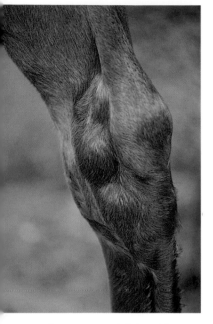

Lumps over a joint could indicate the early stages of arthritis.

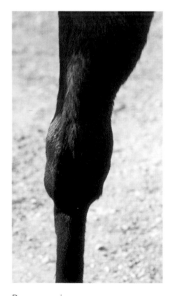

Bone spavin.

spavin formation and can be seen in routine hock X-rays in a sound horse.

Lameness is characteristic of the early inflammatory stages of spavin formation, and the musculature in the horse's back end will tighten up to support the weakness in the hocks. A qualified equine physiotherapist will be able to help by releasing this muscle spasm, so making the horse less stiff and better able to work through from behind. However, as long as there is an underlying structural problem – the development of spavins – the muscle spasm will keep returning.

With regard to work, depending on your vet's advice as to how much work the horse can sustain without pain, walk poles and slightly raised trotting poles will increase joint flexion and the production of better quality joint fluid. It is believed that one of the causes of spavin is that the joints involved have a very small range of movement, and this is insufficient to stimulate healthy cartilage development and nutrition.

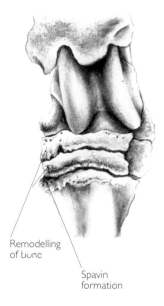

Remodelling of bone

Spavin formation

Work over poles, such as this T Team exercise, will increase joint flexion and may help to ease the stiffness associated with bone spavin.

Top tips

- Feed a supplement containing glucosamine and chondroitin, as these compounds have been shown to promote cartilage healing and protection.
- Sore joints will benefit from a degree of exercise. However, too much will cause pain and hasten further degeneration. Follow your vet's advice. Horses with arthritis cope better if they are turned out as much as possible, so they can gently exercise themselves as they graze.
- If you are still able to ride your horse, little and often is best. Stick to hacking out, rather than schooling, and work mainly in straight lines as circles and bends will put additional strain on joints. Preferably, the ground should not be too hard and you should avoid prolonged periods of trotting on hard or uneven surfaces.
- Do not allow your horse to put on weight, as this will overload a sore joint and make the situation worse.

If this work increases the horse's discomfort, the only course of action is to wait until the spavins have settled. As long as the bones in the joint fuse with no spurs (projections of bone), there is no reason why the horse should not become sound again and return to normal work.

Treatment

There are many treatment options available and your vet will decide which is the most appropriate, depending on the severity of the injury and the joint involved. If the joint is badly sprained and showing only an enlarged joint capsule, such as you might see in a windgall, applying ice packs and giving anti-inflammatory medication and rest may be all that is needed.

Occasionally, an inflamed joint may be flushed arthroscopically. This is where a narrow tube is inserted into the joint via a small incision. Where it can be justified, this has the advantage of flushing out inflammatory debris, fatigued synovial fluid, blood and any cartilage breakdown products. This greatly improves the healing response, but financial considerations usually limit this procedure to the most severely damaged joints.

There is a small range of drugs with which to treat joints. The first, and perhaps most widely used, are the corticosteroids. These are potent anti-inflammatory drugs which reduce synovitis and protect cartilage from the harmful effects of inflammatory waste products. There has long been a fear that steroids lead to further joint damage – however, this is not the case unless they are overused or the joint is not given the appropriate rest.

Hyaluronic acid, a compound found naturally in synovial fluid, can also help. It has a marked effect in reducing inflammation within joints and can be injected intravenously or directly into the joint. It is often injected into a joint in combination with a corticosteroid.

A group of compounds called polysulphated glucosaminoglycans are also widely used to treat joint disease. These extracts, or synthetic components, of cartilage can help to repair damaged articular cartilage. They can be used as a dietary supplement or injected directly into a joint.

Early recognition and rest are vital to ensure joint recovery and to give medication an opportunity to work. If your horse injures a joint, don't rush him back into work as soon as it looks better, as such injuries can easily recur. In these cases, patience will be rewarded.

Added extras

- Cod liver oil has been used in the horse world for a long time and can be of significant benefit to the older, arthritic horse. It should be fed at a rate of approximately 15–30ml (1–2 tablespoons) daily. Cider vinegar is also fed by a number of people at similar dose rates (up to 50ml/3 tablespoons daily), but its effect is less certain.
- Copper bands are a common lay treatment for arthritis. The only problem with using them on horses is the risk of trauma to the skin and the horse catching the band on something while grazing. But appropriate precautions can help to reduce these risks.
- Magnetic devices are popular in the horse world for helping with joint problems. These are also attached to the horse (usually by means of bandages, boots or rugs) and could, therefore, potentially carry the same risks as copper bands. Some people claim they have a dramatic effect.

Clicking joints

A clicking noise in the joints is often created by very small vacuums being formed in the joint fluid which then move and dissipate. In themselves they do not point to any joint problems and the noise can come from any normal joint. However, in an older horse clicking hocks may signify that arthritis is becoming a problem, so follow the advice for dealing with this condition.

In the pastern, clicking can be generated by partial dislocation of the pastern joint: the long pastern bone extends further than the short pastern bone and then clicks back into place. This can be seen if you watch the pastern joint from the side.

The condition can cause discomfort for the horse and is also a cosmetic problem. A procedure to lower the heel of the foot concerned, plus controlled exercise, will usually correct the problem.

Magnetic leg and hock wraps.

Navicular syndrome – bursitis and navicular disease

Navicular bursitis is one of the most common causes of chronic or longstanding forelimb lameness in horses. Although the symptoms may vary from horse to horse, we see an inflammatory reaction, mainly in the navicular bursa, but also in the navicular bone, causing pain and dysfunction.

Navicular disease is a very much rarer but incurable form of navicular syndrome, and is a progressive, degenerative osteopathy of the navicular bone. It occurs typically in young horses in the early stages of their career.

Navicular syndrome is of one of two main problems affecting the navicular bone. The other is fracture of the bone (see page 137), although the first condition may lead to the second.

The navicular bone

This small, boat-shaped bone can cause tremendous problems to the horse. It lies deep within the hoof and nestles behind the last two bones in the foot (the distal phalanges). It is a type of bone known as a sesamoid and there are a number of these bones in the limbs. Their function is to act as a fulcrum to facilitate tendon leverage, particularly in the early stages of movement when a limb is either flexed or extended.

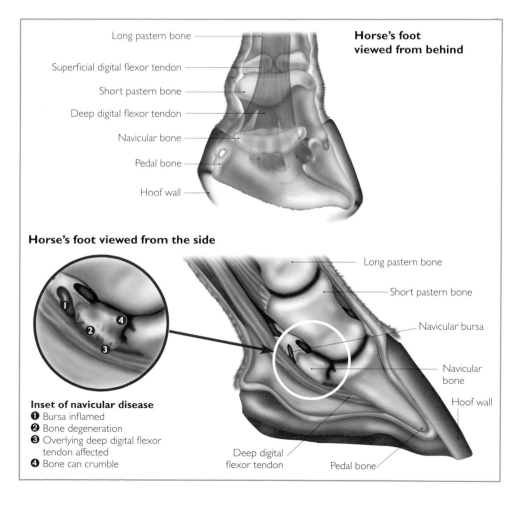

Horse's foot viewed from behind

Long pastern bone
Superficial digital flexor tendon
Short pastern bone
Deep digital flexor tendon
Navicular bone
Pedal bone
Hoof wall

Horse's foot viewed from the side

Long pastern bone
Short pastern bone
Navicular bursa
Navicular bone
Hoof wall
Deep digital flexor tendon
Pedal bone

Inset of navicular disease
❶ Bursa inflamed
❷ Bone degeneration
❸ Overlying deep digital flexor tendon affected
❹ Bone can crumble

The tendon involved in this case is the deep digital flexor tendon. To find this, run your hand up from the fetlock behind the front leg until you can feel the taut, bar-like tendons. There are clearly two. The deep digital flexor tendon is the inner one of these. A small bag of fluid lies between this tendon and the navicular bone. This is called the navicular bursa.

Navicular disease attacks the bone and eats into it, generally on the rear surface, causing hollows and cavities to appear. Disintegration of the bone produces chronic and persistent pain.

Symptoms

Navicular syndrome is a progressive forelimb lameness, developing over many months. It is a condition with many different early signs, which can be difficult to spot. Recurrent bruising of the sole on the affected feet may signal a problem. This is because affected horses tend to throw more weight on to their toes to avoid navicular pain. Vague, uncertain, and on-and-off periods of forelimb discomfort may be an indicator.

Horses with navicular often have boxy feet.

Although the problem may appear to be in one limb only, it is usually in both forefeet but it is difficult for a horse to demonstrate classical signs of lameness in both forelegs at the same time. The less severely affected leg will mask the severity of the signs of the other limb. Even in quite advanced disease, lameness may seem relatively mild, but the gait is strange and pottery. Sudden, severe unilateral lameness may occur when one navicular bone weakens and fractures. The fracture is the last straw and a sequel to an undiagnosed problem.

As navicular syndrome progresses the feet change shape, again because the horse throws his weight on to the front of the foot to ease the pain. The foot grows smaller, narrower and higher in the heel. It becomes more boxy, the sole becomes abnormally concave and the frog gets smaller. Therefore, it is useful to compare the size of the two front feet.

Causes

Navicular syndrome is seen in horses typically between four and six years of age. There is usually a history of overwork and too frequent exercise, particularly on hard ground. Poor quality foot trimming can also add to the problem.

The exact causes of navicular syndrome are not fully understood, but we know that it is seen when there is poor conformation or repetitive trauma to the foot. There are three main ideas on what happens:

■ Inadequate blood supply reaching the navicular bone causes weakness.
■ Abnormal stress placed on the bursa and the bone by the overlying tendon causes inflammation and decay.
■ Degeneration of the bone and surrounding tissue leads to arthritic change.

Diagnosis

The visual signs are usually enough to lead you to suspect navicular syndrome. Clinical evaluation will show pain over the centre of the frog. Your vet will need to determine whether this is bursitis or, more seriously, navicular disease.

Radiography is a useful next step and will identify classic bone changes typical of navicular disease, but the results must be viewed as part of the picture rather than the whole story. A diagnostic imaging technique called nuclear scintigraphy will identify early inflammatory changes before physical changes occur to the bone, although it is expensive.

Treatment

No treatment is effective in true navicular disease. Treatment of navicular bursitis involves:

■ Good farriery. Correction of any foot imbalance is important. The goal is to create a wide, long and raised heel and a short toe. Supportive shoeing is also useful. In the early stages of

What conformation is prone to navicular?

Navicular syndrome is often seen in horses with:
■ Upright pasterns, with long toes and low heels.
■ Small feet in relation to body size.
■ Side-to-side imbalance in the foot.
■ Sheared heels.

What else could it be?

Navicular syndrome may not be the obvious cause of lameness at the beginning, due to the insidious nature of the condition. Other conditions that initially look similar are:
■ Puncture of the sole.
■ Fracture of the pedal bone.
■ Pedal osteitis.
■ Ringbone.
■ Laminitis.
The truth of the matter frequently becomes apparent as time passes and the condition progresses.

Corrective shoeing is often used to treat horses with navicular syndrome. An egg-bar shoe can be used to protect the navicular area following a fracture.

the disease, good farriery and gently increasing exercise may be enough to stabilize the situation.

- Use of corticosteroids, which are injected into the bursa.
- Judicious use of non-steroidal anti-inflammatory drugs, such as bute, will relieve the inflammation and pain. These can be particularly useful if used a day or so before any anticipated work. It must be remembered that these drugs are not curative and their effects must not be abused.
- Chondroprotective agents aid repair of the cartilage covering the navicular bone and can be helpful.
- A number of surgical options exist. Certain ligaments may be surgically cut to change the pressures on the navicular bone (navicular suspensory desmotomy), thereby reducing the pain. Although this approach has promise, any improvements are unlikely to be long term.

Alternatively, nerves supplying the area may be cut to block sensation in the bone (neurectomy). This technique is palliative (it lessens pain but does not offer a cure) an must be regarded as a last resort. Unfortunately, the loss of sensation that occurs after a neurectomy may, with overwork, hasten the deterioration of the navicular bone.

Avoiding navicular

There are a few simple ways to minimize the chance of your horse developing the condition:

- Buy a horse with good conformation, particularly the feet, and a known background, who has a sensible work profile in the years prior to purchase.
- Make sure your horse has good and regular farriery.
- Do not allow your horse to get fat. If he becomes overweight he will be placing more strain on his joints and skeletal frame.
- Avoid over-strenuous training.
- Provide adequate rest for your horse following any injury.
- Do not breed from a horse with navicular disease or one with poor conformation.

Navicular bone fracture

A fracture of the navicular bone is a serious injury that can lead to permanent lameness. However, fractures that occur in the hind foot are a little more forgiving and there is a potential for soundness, on paddock rest at least.

The horse will show sudden, acute lameness. In most cases hindlimb fractures occur as a result of the horse kicking the stable wall, but the crisis can occur as a result of navicular disease. X-rays will provide a definitive diagnosis.

The reasons for the poor outlook are the constant movement of the overlying tendon causing instability, and the fact that the navicular bone usually does not heal with a firm bone-to-bone union. Instead it heals with just a fibrous bond between the fragments. When the bone comes under pressure, movement can take place, which causes pain.

The main way to help your horse at this time is through special shoeing. An egg-bar shoe will protect and take pressure off the navicular area. A shoe of this round type will have to be applied indefinitely, and changed on a regular basis, depending on hoof growth. Your farrier will be able to advise you further.

You will need to give the horse a long period of rest at grass – between six months and one year – with regular examinations by your vet to assess the degree of lameness. Do not allow the horse to get too fat as this will increase pressure on the damaged bone. In addition, feed supplements containing a source of glucosamine and chondroitin may be beneficial.

Surgery may resolve the problem in selected cases, but sadly some cases fail to respond at all. Healing is easy to judge as soundness returns and X-rays will reveal good bony healing. If a fracture is a sequel to degenerative navicular disease, euthanasia is usually the only option.

New drug treatment for navicular

A new drug may offer some hope for horses with navicular, although initial results have proved disappointing. Tildren, currently licensed in some countries but not others, has offered the chance to keep horses with navicular in regular work and pain-free.

In normal circumstances, bones are always remodelling themselves. Some bone cells remove bone at the same time as other cells produce more bone, but a healthy balance is always maintained.

With navicular, more bone is destroyed than produced, and hollows and cavities appear, leading to general weakness. The drug works by rebalancing this – it inhibits the cells that destroy the bone, therefore allowing new bone-producing cells to flourish.

The drug also works to stop the symptoms re-emerging in horses that have already been diagnosed. Tildren is thought to be most effective if given within six months of diagnosis. The prognosis is not as good if the deep digital flexor tendon is already damaged.

Pedal osteitis

Pedal osteitis is a condition where the pedal bone changes shape as a result of wear and tear over quite a long period. It is typically identified in large, flat-footed horses, whose feet have been allowed to flare. There is little that can be done to reverse the degenerative changes within the pedal bone. The only options are painkillers to make the horse more comfortable and possibly packing within the shoe to provide some protection.

Correcting hoof shape with good farriery is the most effective therapy. It is also possible for a vet or farrier to apply a firm, rubber-like resin hoof-filler to the sole of the foot, filling the space formed by the shoe, to cushion and protect the structures of the foot.

Sesamoiditis

Sesamoiditis is a condition that affects the two small bones positioned behind each fetlock joint. It is more usual for the front fetlocks to be affected, and the condition usually occurs after the horse has performed some strenuous work on hard ground. It shows as lameness affecting one of the front legs, with heat, swelling and pain over a sesamoid bone. Pressing on the swollen area evokes a pain response and an increase in the severity of the lameness. Often, the other front sesamoids will show some tenderness as well when pressed.

On X-rays, the condition shows as wide-open channels in the sesamoid bone, radiating out towards the surface of the bone. In old cases of this disease, extra new bone can be seen on the outside surface of the affected sesamoid.

Unfortunately, sesamoiditis is a disease that can recur whenever work is done, especially on hard ground, even after prolonged rest and treatment. Anti-inflammatory treatment will help to allow the horse back into light work such as hacking. The amount of hard work he will be able to stand varies from case to case and you should ask your vet for advice.

Strenuous work on hard ground can trigger a bout of sesamoiditis.

Locking stifle

In order to rest standing up, horses have a method of locking the stifle joint by means of hooking the inside (medial) ligament of the patella (kneecap) over a bony ridge of the femur. When the horse wants to move, he contracts the muscles that lift up the patella and this releases the ligament from the bone.

In some horses, this unlocking mechanism does not work smoothly and the characteristic locking of the joint continues as the horse moves. This gives rise to a dramatic dragging of the straight hindleg until the patella finally disentangles itself and, suddenly, all is well. When it returns to normal the horse is usually perfectly sound. The problem usually occurs after a period of rest but in bad cases it can occur during movement and exercise.

This condition is known as upward fixation of the patella (locking stifle) and tends to affect young, unfit horses, thin horses, and those with poor muscle development on their thighs and/or straight hindleg conformation. Usually the problem is transitory and will not cause arthritis to occur in later life.

Exercising on hills will improve hindleg muscle tone and help to resolve the problem of a locking stifle.

In the vast majority of cases, gradually increasing levels of exercise (particularly hill work) will build up muscle tone in the large muscle above the patella, allowing easier unlocking to occur and abolishing the condition. If your horse is in poor condition, increasing his food will build up the fat pad beneath the patella, again allowing unlocking to occur.

In some cases the medial ligament of the patella can be cut surgically, which will alleviate the condition. However, many vets prefer to reserve this operation for cases that do not respond to exercise and in fact it is rarely performed.

A double movement in the horse's shoulder can be worrying, but may be simply a quirk of conformation.

Double movement of the shoulder

With this condition, the horse's shoulder appears to move or jar further than it should. Any apparent discrepancy in movement like this can be very worrying, but if the horse is not lame and is performing well this double movement can be put down simply to conformation.

If your horse displays this peculiarity, ask your vet to check that he is definitely not lame or showing other signs of joint problems. If everything is fine, carry on enjoying your horse.

Mud fever

Every season brings its own set of potential health problems and the wet weather of autumn and winter is no exception. One of the most common is mud fever – also known as greasy heel or cracked heels (scratches or rain rot in the USA) – and is usually found on the horse's coronet, pastern and heels, but sometimes on the belly or even the neck, commonly in horses with white legs, pink skin or heavy feathering. Rain scald is a similar condition that appears on the horse's back and neck.

Mud fever is caused by the bacterium *Dermatophilus congolenesis*, which loves damp, muddy weather as this provides the conditions it needs to thrive. Added to this, continual wetting of the horse's skin weakens its surface, and any resulting abrasions allow the bacteria in. The micro-organism lives in soil, where it can survive for years waiting for an opportunity to penetrate chapped or soft, vulnerable skin. This explains why a horse may not suffer from mud fever in one field, but when moved to another (perhaps less muddy) field will develop the condition.

Horses are more vulnerable to mud fever when recovering from illness, if they are sweating profusely, if they have sore areas or if they are sharing tack with an infected horse. Horses whose legs are washed daily with forceful water jets can develop chapped skin, which is perfect for bacteria to penetrate.

White legs are usually more prone to mud fever, which shows up as sore, scabby areas.

Symptoms

The signs of mud fever can vary from horse to horse. In long-haired animals the hair is often matted and, when parted, reveals scabs and a smelly, jelly-like pus. Skin underneath the scabs will be sore and thickened. When the scab is gently removed, new hair protrudes through the skin underneath with a paintbrush effect. In short-haired animals the scabs are smaller and feel more like tiny lumps or seeds in the coat. Some of the hair will be patchy and raised, giving a rather moth-eaten appearance.

The horse may also be tender in the area and reluctant to let you touch him. There may be heat and swelling, and in severe cases he could go lame. Mud fever can develop into a serious bacterial infection, so it is worth calling out your vet if you think your horse has the condition.

Treatment

Mud fever requires diligence, patience and regular treatment over a long period to achieve the best results.

Cleansing

Begin by soaking and washing the sore areas with an antiseptic shampoo or lotion, which will kill off the bacteria and make removal of infected scabs easier. Clipping away any excessive feathering will make it easier to clean up the area, but avoid clipping the legs if you can.

Removing scabs

Getting air to the area will kill the bacteria so it is better for the scabs to be removed – but this is best done by softening them, not picking them off, which may be painful for the horse. There are a number of preparations

Be vigilant over winter and watch out for sore spots on your horse's heels.

Progress of the condition

Once mud fever occurs, gradually as the affected area swells, the horse's skin stretches and starts to weep. After a while, cracks appear in the skin and the hair on the surrounding area falls out. Often crusts form as the weepy secretion dries and glues the strands of hair together, forming hard, scabby lumps. If the scabs are removed, areas of moist pink skin lie underneath. These are often raised and round in shape. If the infection continues it will progress from the bulbs of the heel, gradually creeping round to the front of the fetlock and pastern areas.

When the horse moves, the cracks in the skin can open up, leading to pain and discomfort. In the most severe cases, the horse may go lame and the legs often swell. Secondary complications can follow, including bacterial infection with *Staphylococci*, *Streptococci* or *Corynebacteria*. In the most severe cases, badly affected areas may even have a foul, putrid odour.

Preventing mud fever

- Rotate grazing so that fields do not become poached, or tackle mud in gateways by putting down hardcore.
- Stable your horse more frequently in wetter conditions, especially if he is prone to mud fever.
- Use a pair of special boots or leg wraps to avoid mud getting on to the skin.

Turnout boots that cover the horse's heels may help to prevent mud fever.

- Use some of the barrier products available to keep mud away from the skin.
- Avoid hosing mud from your horse's legs. Instead, allow it to dry and then brush it off.
- When stabling your horse, make sure that his bedding is clean and dry.

available to help soften scabs and allow them to drop off. Wear gloves and dispose of any debris very carefully as the bacteria can survive in infected crusts for several years.

Drying

After cleaning, dry the legs thoroughly with a soft towel.

Topical treatment

In milder cases, simply apply a layer of Vaseline or a soothing lanolin salve to act as a barrier. More severe cases will benefit from an antibiotic cream or other product designed to soothe soreness and tackle bacteria. Follow the product instructions or speak to your vet. Special boots designed to go under the heel and create a barrier against mud may also be useful.

Continue treatment daily for about a week, removing any scabs that re-form, then continue twice-weekly until the condition has cleared up. If the condition worsens, or the horse develops lameness or leg swelling, you should consult your vet who may prescribe a course of antibiotics and anti-inflammatories.

Filled legs and lymphangitis

Some stabled horses develop swollen or 'filled' legs. There may be accompanying stiffness, but no lameness. However, within a short time of being turned out or ridden, the swelling subsides.

The reason that horses' legs fill in this way is that fluid from the blood vessels leaks out into the surrounding tissue too easily and is not carried away quickly enough by the lymph vessels. Nobody knows why this happens more in some horses than others, but treatment involves providing more opportunity for exercise and ideally a larger stable so that the horse can move around.

Lymphangitis is a related but more serious condition involving infection, and can be a complication of a chronic case of filled legs or mud fever. It can also result from an infected wound that has gone unnoticed, with the infection passing through the lymph system to cause painful swelling of the entire limb and oozing of fluid. The horse will be extremely lame and have a high temperature.

Treatment involves antibiotics to counteract the infection, plus diuretics and anti-inflammatories to reduce the swelling. Once a horse has suffered from lymphangitis he will be more prone to further episodes, especially if exercise is restricted or he is allowed to get too fat.

Tendon problems

Tendons are dense, fibrous structures that are very strong but not very elastic. They transmit muscle energy, particularly from the well-developed chest and hindquarter muscles, down through the legs, giving the horse his power and speed. As tendons age they become even less stretchy, and as this occurs they are less able to repair themselves if damaged.

Case study: Photosensitization

In spring and summer my horse has a problem with swollen pasterns and heels. The skin seems to erupt, which makes walking painful, and my vet has diagnosed photosensitization. My horse is given antibiotic and anti-inflammatory injections, and when the healing process starts huge scabs form up to the cannon bone. I would appreciate any advice.

Photosensitization takes two forms, either primary or secondary. The plants that cause primary photosensitization include buckwheat, St John's wort, bishop's weed and parsley. Secondary photosensitization involves liver damage and your vet can take a blood sample to confirm whether this is the case with your horse.

The condition occurs systemically. This means the plant is ingested and chlorophyll pigment circulates in the blood, causing photosensitization of the skin throughout the whole body. Sunlight is also required for photosensitization to take place, so the areas of skin that are not protected by pigment (that is, where there are white markings) are those that will be affected.

Various other forms of dermatitis, or inflammation of the skin, can result from contact irritation of the lower legs. This can be caused by rough pasture, or occasionally harvest mites, or a combination of contact irritation and sunburn. The most appropriate treatment may therefore be to rule out harvest mite infestation, use a sunblock and, if at all possible, try to move your horse to improved pasture to remove the source of offending plants.

Facts about tendon injuries

- Recovery is always long term: after the initial injury, healing does not occur to any real degree until the 120-day mark, then it progresses at a slow rate. A total of 12–18 months is usual and involves many weeks of box rest.
- Usually, the horse cannot be turned out fully until between six and nine months following the initial injury.
- Tendons heal by forming scar tissue – not by making new tendon tissue.
- As a result, the healed tendon is often stiffer and less flexible than it was before the injury.
- This causes more strain on the remaining tendon tissue when it is put under pressure, so the risk of re-injury following recovery is quite high.

Causes

Tendon injuries occur when individual fibres are torn or ruptured and it is not always easy to predict how this might happen. Causes can include:

- Direct injury, for example from an overreach inflicted by another leg.
- Too much weight being put on the leg, perhaps when galloping or jumping.
- A horse being exercised beyond his level of fitness.
- A burst of explosive energy and sudden strain as the horse gallops loose in the field.
- Occasionally, overtight boots or bandages.

Tendon injuries occur in a variety of situations, including when excess weight is put on a leg during jumping.

Symptoms

Tendon injuries can vary in their intensity, but even mild ones are worth watching out for – if you exercise a horse with a mild tendon injury before it has healed, you will probably make the condition worse. Mild tendon injuries tend to show up as increased heat and a slight temporary thickening of the leg, but the horse may not always be lame. However, the area may be tender if gently squeezed.

If the injury is severe there will be pain, heat and swelling as the tendon fibres will be completely ruptured, and the horse will be obviously lame.

An ultrasound scan is the best way to determine the degree of injury, but be guided by your vet as to the best time to do this. Scanning a day or two after a suspected problem may only show minor damage, but 7–10 days later the defect may appear much worse as scar tissue forms and healing progresses. The classic tendon injury will show up on a scan as a hole in the core of the tendon. Tears and splits can also be revealed by a scan.

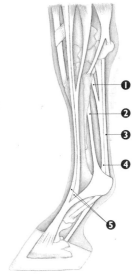

There is no muscle, or flesh, to protect the tendons in the lower limb, so they are much more likely to be damaged by an injury or blow to the leg.

❶ Check ligament
❷ Suspensory ligament
❸ Superficial digital flexor tendon
❹ Deep digital flexor tendon
❺ Extensor tendons

Treatment

If you suspect your horse has injured a tendon, fast action can make all the difference to his recovery. Phone the vet and use cold hosing or therapy to try to reduce the heat and inflammation that can cause further internal damage. Your vet will be able to advise about the use of anti-inflammatories, if appropriate, and careful bandaging. Therapeutic ultrasound may also help, and some vets like to consider other treatments such as laser therapy or even traditional tendon firing.

Another treatment that has recently been found useful is tendon splitting – better described these days as tendon stabbing. This option involves multiple, fan-like incisions into the tendon through small skin punctures, which allow the area of injury to drain and help promote healing. It is performed on a standing, sedated horse under local anaesthetic.

Box rest will be required, sometimes for lengthy periods,

Avoiding tendon problems

- Build up work very slowly over a period of months.
- Start with slow work in walk over varied terrain and use uphill if possible.
- Get your farrier to check hoof balance.
- Try not to use boots all the time, unless unavoidable.
- Always allow tendons and legs to warm up before exercise and cool down afterwards.

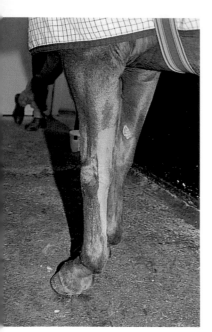

followed by controlled turnout. You must be advised by your vet, after a thorough examination of the tendon, as to when this takes place as it is a crucial time in the recovery process. A small yard or small area of a field fenced off by electric fencing is ideal. This will give your horse space to walk around outside, but will not be big enough to allow lots of trotting or any canter or gallop. This should be home for your horse for two months, before you turn him out into a field. The tendon can be examined by ultrasound on a regular basis by your vet to tell you how the healing is progressing. Patience is needed to allow the best healing possible. Once a tendon has settled, it usually stops hurting and painkillers can be halted.

Tendon injuries need plenty of time to heal properly.

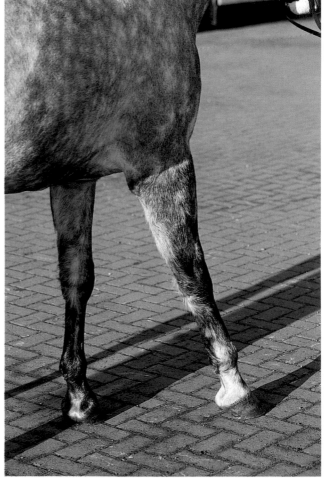

Using bone marrow

The newest treatment of all is also one of the most exciting. At present, the main problem with recovery is that a horse's tendons actually contain relatively few cells – particularly in mature horses. This means there are usually too few cells available for damage repair.

Bone marrow has a unique part to play in cell regeneration and damage repair, in that its cells have no specific function other than to develop into a range of tissue types. One of its primary roles is to act as a nursery for repair cells, which can then be released on demand to repair or replace tissue within the body as and when required.

The blood supply to a horse's tendons is too poor to be able to provide enough of these repair cells via natural means, so it seems logical to inject bone marrow cells into the site of the injury. Unfortunately, when this technique was tried it resulted in some undesirable side effects, probably because of the wide range of cell types which are included in the bone marrow sample. Vets involved in this research have sought to improve the technique by separating the different marrow cells and using only the most appropriate type.

This process is begun by harvesting bone marrow from the horse's sternum; for this procedure the horse can be conscious but sedated. Once harvested, the cells are separated and the most appropriate cells allowed to multiply in a lab until there are enough of them to treat the tendon – this usually takes around a month. After this an ultrasound scanner is used to guide the cells accurately into place through injection into the leg – the horse need only be sedated for this procedure. Scanning again at a later date shows that the tendons repair themselves more quickly using this method than would be expected with more conventional treatment.

This technique is expensive, not yet widely available and to an extent still at an experimental stage. Not every tendon injury will be suitable for this treatment, either: scanning needs to reveal an obvious 'hole' in the tendon otherwise there will be no area into which to inject the new cells.

Box rest

Your vet might prescribe box rest for all sorts of reasons and the amount your horse will need varies with each individual and the particular problem. A small wound may mean only a couple of days in the stable but something more major, like recovery from tendon injuries, can involve months of confinement.

The aim of box rest is simple: to restrict movement so that the horse has the best chance of recovery. You may hate the idea of it, but your vet's recommendations should always be followed – failure to do so could mean a lengthy setback.

However, if your horse is really not settling he may hurt himself more on box rest than he would in the field. In these cases it is important to get your vet's advice – he may suggest using a small paddock or fenced concrete area. If this is not an option, sedation may be useful as a short-term measure to keep your horse calm.

Keep him comfortable

Depending on your horse's injury, you may need to alter his bedding. For example, a pony with acute laminitis will need a deep, comfy bed but this would not be suitable for a horse wearing thick leg bandages. Many horses on prolonged box rest do well on rubber matting with bedding at a thickness to suit the injury. It is an expensive option if you do not have the matting already, but seek advice from your vet if you are not sure what to do.

Your horse's feet will need to be picked out twice a day to prevent thrush and other foot-related problems.

It is vital your horse does not become dehydrated, so monitor his drinking and change his water twice a day. If he is not drinking much, try offering him water that has been warmed slightly – many horses find this a bit more tempting.

Monitor your horse's droppings. Any change in them can be one of the first signs that he is not coping with his situation.

Feeding

Once your horse is on box rest and receiving no exercise, you will obviously need to be careful with his feeding.

Fibre first

The majority of your horse's diet should be fibre-based, ideally hay or haylage, which will also help to keep him occupied. Try

Company

Is your horse more or less stressed by being able to see other horses? Some become very stressed while others take comfort from it. You may need to move him into a different stable to accommodate his needs. If your horse gets stressed seeing other horses through his stable windows, consider blacking them out. Is there a horse on the yard he has a strong bond with? Ask the owner if he can stay in for an extra hour or so a day to keep your horse company. If he is within touching distance, even better.

Having a friend nearby can help some horses cope with box rest.

Top feeding tips

If your horse is stressed or depressed, here are some tips to get him to eat:

- Offer very small but regular feeds – large feeds may put him off.
- Add succulents such as apples or carrots to his feed to tempt him.
- If your horse is turned off his food because of the smell of medicines, try adding garlic to mask them.
- Make sure the feed bowl is in a good position and does not cause stress to his injury.
- Leave your horse to enjoy his feed, and don't rush him to finish it.

If your vet permits it, grazing your horse in-hand for short periods will cheer him up.

small-hole haynets hung in different places around the stable to extend feeding time and encourage natural browsing.

Avoid radical changes

Remember the golden rule: 'Feed according to work done'. If your horse is on box rest, even for a few days, he is not doing his usual work and should be fed accordingly. Do not make radical changes – stick with his usual feeds but change the amounts fed. Increase the level of fibre and decrease the amount of higher energy concentrates, adding a general-purpose vitamin and mineral supplement. If he is to be on long-term box rest, you could consider gradually changing to a lower energy concentrate and lower energy chaff.

Stress-free

Temperament can often be a problem for horses on box rest. If your horse is stressed, then you need to consider adding a calming supplement.

Free radical toxins can exaggerate and prolong stress – if you add a supplement with natural antioxidants, this will flush out free radicals from his system and help your horse restore a healthy balance.

Beat boredom

Stable toys will help to prevent boredom and depression setting in and avoid your horse developing vices, which are seen all too often in stabled horses. If cost is an issue, tie a swede or turnip on to baler twine and hang it from the stable roof or door. Your horse will spend ages trying to eat it. Leave carrots or other treats in the bedding – he will enjoy rooting them out.

Visit your horse as much as you can. Twice daily visits are the norm for most owners, but consider a third visit in the middle of the day. Your horse will appreciate the company and a groom or massage at the same time will go down a treat.

If your vet will allow it, and your horse won't go ballistic, leading him out to graze in-hand will be a very welcome break.

If your horse is prescribed a long period of box rest, you may need to assess whether your yard is the best place for him to be. If there is no one around during the day, you may need to move him – if only temporarily. If your horse needs attention in the day, it is reassuring to know there is someone around to see to him or give you a call if needed.

Back to normal

It might not seem like it at the time, but box rest *will* come to an end. However, your horse's return to his normal routine needs to be handled carefully. How this is done will depend on his temperament and how long he has been on box rest.

Initially, your vet will probably ask you to walk him out in-hand – usually twice a day at first. You may find your horse is very lively, so use appropriate equipment (see panel). This will help to stop him pulling away. Brushing boots will help to protect his legs. Gloves and a hard hat are a must for you.

If he is particularly lively, your vet may use a small amount of sedation and even suggest that you ride him instead of leading him – this can be a safer option as it offers more control.

When turning your horse out for the first time, do it in a small 'recovery' paddock if possible, and find a quiet, well-mannered horse to keep him company. You will probably have to limit turnout to a couple of hours a day at first and, again, your vet may use sedation to keep your horse as calm as possible over the first few days.

Wait until he is completely calm when turned out before reintroducing him to the herd. Your vet will advise you on when to do this. Your horse will need to be brought back into work slowly and you should follow a proper fittening regime to prevent further injury. An instructor or your vet will be able to help you with this.

Top management tips

- Make the stable environment as dust-free as possible. Consider switching from straw bedding to an alternative, and use haylage or soak his hay.
- Try apple bobbing. A few apples in a bucket of water can keep your horse busy for ages – until he works out that if he drinks all the water the apples are there for the taking!
- Do easy neck-stretch exercises with a treat your horse likes, getting him to take the treat from each flank and from between his forelegs. Lift and stretch each foreleg in turn, forward and back to help free his shoulders and lower neck.
- Use wraps or sausage boots to protect his legs unless this goes against your vet's advice. They will need to be taken off every eight hours and his legs given a good rub.
- Make sure your horse's rugs fit well if he is going to be wearing them 24 hours a day, and adjust them regularly to prevent irritation.
- Groom your horse vigorously for 40 minutes a day to help improve his muscle tone.
- When it is time to start walking him out, take him in the school. Walking him in an open space may lead to mischief! If you are worried about control initially, use a bridle, roller and side reins, or two people each leading from a lunge line.
- Save turning your horse out fully until he can be ridden. You can then tire him a little before letting him loose in the field.

Protecting your horse's legs

There is a wide range of boots available to protect your horse's legs from almost any injury he is likely to receive while being ridden.

Brushing boots

Very few horses are totally straight and most will brush or dish slightly. A horse will brush because of his static conformation (when the skeletal system is not moving) or his dynamic conformation (when the limbs are in motion).

A horse with slightly toe-out or cow-hock conformation will usually brush. Brushing boots will help prevent self-inflicted injuries from the other limb (many people use them as a standard piece of tack), but if a horse brushes low down he may need coronet boots.

Brushing boots are mainly worn for flatwork, hacking or turning out for short periods. They can be used for jumping but do not give as much protection to the front legs as tendon or cross-country boots (see overleaf). If a horse has a tendency to strike his knee or hock, a speedicut boot would be a better option as it protects higher up the leg.

If your horse's shoes are striking each other, talk to your farrier about the best type of shoes to prevent this happening. Normally, the farrier will round off the inside edge of the shoes to help stop them brushing together.

Fetlock boots

Fetlock boots, also known as quarter boots, are a shorter alternative to brushing boots and are worn on the hind fetlocks to protect the joint. They are often used by experienced riders for showjumping to encourage the horse to be careful. They can be worn for hacking and light schooling, but not for cross-country as they do not provide enough protection around the cannon bone and tendons.

Safety boots

There are now boots on the market that aim to prevent shoes being pulled off. They are also designed to protect the heel from a strike of the hindleg and aid blood circulation around the leg when the frog comes into contact with the bar. The boots can be used for any discipline, even when wearing studs or when the horse is turned out in the field, and are suitable for horses wearing special shoes for medical reasons.

Putting on overreach (bell) boots

Turn the boot inside out and pick up the horse's front foot – hold it between your knees like a farrier does, so that both your hands are free.

Alternatively, hold the hoof with one hand and pull the boot on with the other. Pull the boot over the foot, toe first.

Once the boot is in place, turn it the right way out. To take the boot off again, grab the top and pull down, so that the boot slides off over the bulb of the heel first.

Overreach boots

Overreach boots fit over the coronet and heel to protect the horse's foot. Horses are more likely to overreach – strike into the back of a front foot with the front of a back one – when jumping, lungeing, in transit or in muddy conditions, and this can lead to a nasty injury. If your horse forges (the clicking you can sometimes hear when the back shoes hits the front shoe), he is more susceptible to an overreach.

Overreach boots come in various designs, the most common being a simple, one-piece rubber bell – which can be fiddly to put on (see panel). Boots with touch-and-close or strap fastenings are also available, but tend to be more expensive than the rubber bell-type. Petal overreach boots – which have rows of 'petals' attached to a strap that fastens around the pastern – are also available, although this type makes a flapping sound that takes some getting used to. Whichever type you choose, make sure the boots are not too big, or the horse might trip over them.

Tendon boots

Tendon boots are designed to protect the tendons at the back of the horse's foreleg from being struck into by the hindleg when showjumping. Contrary to what many people think, tendon boots are not intended to support the tendon.

When buying tendon boots, look for designs with a cut-away or flexible area behind the knee to ensure that no restriction is placed on the horse's ability to flex fully while jumping.

Cross-country boots

The correct protective equipment for your horse is vital when you are riding cross-country. His legs are most vulnerable – he could hit a fence, strike into himself, or overstretch a tendon or ligament while competing. Cross-country boots offer protection against these injuries.

There are different schools of thought on how much protection boots should provide. Some say you should protect the horse's legs completely with boots that are reinforced in the vulnerable areas. Others say the horse needs only minimal protection, so that he knows what it feels like to hit a fence and therefore respects it and jumps carefully, and some boots are designed with this in mind.

When a horse gallops or lands after a fence, his fetlock joint extends to its limit, touching the ground in some cases. Certain designs of boot help to reduce the chance of the tendons overextending, and protect the fetlock from concussion and bruising.

Turnout boots

Turnout boots are a relatively new idea. They aim to protect the horse's legs from bashes and bangs in the field all year round. They also keep the legs clean, preventing the onset of mud fever in wet and muddy conditions. To provide full protection, the boots need to mould to the shape of the horse's legs and cover as much of the leg and heel area as possible.

Important If your horse suffers with mud fever, make sure his legs are clean before using turnout boots, otherwise the infection may become worse.

Magnetic boots

Magnetic therapy is thought to improve the flow of blood to and from a painful area. It is believed to bring oxygen-rich blood to an injured area and carry away any infected material, although there is no conclusive scientific evidence to prove that magnetic therapy has a positive effect.

Magnets are usually built into magnetic boots and wraps, and are designed to sit next to the major blood vessels – usually on the horse's legs – to encourage bloodflow. Some allow you to fix the magnets in a chosen  place, targeting specific areas. Magnets can help relieve stiffness, improve circulation and disperse swellings. Specific conditions that boots and wraps are believed to help include splints, tendon injuries, suspensory ligament injuries, arthritis, hock and knee damage, windgalls and laminitis.

Soft fluid swellings

Terms such as thoroughpin and windgall strike fear and dread into the mind of horse owners, who worry that such conditions will result in chronic unsoundness. In fact, this is not the case.

An important aspect of any abnormality is first to put the problem into context. The age of the horse is very relevant – what may be considered abnormal in a five-year-old may simply be a sign of natural wear and tear in a 15-year-old. In the older horse, therefore, treatment may be unnecessary and, indeed, is likely to be unsuccessful in many cases.

Lameness, or its absence, must also be considered. Absence of lameness is always reassuring. However, an abnormality may be an early warning sign that should not be ignored if lameness is to be avoided later on.

Demanding equestrian sports such as cross-country riding may cause trauma, resulting in soft fluid swellings.

What is a bursa?

Bursae are small, thin-walled, fluid-filled sacs located at many sites in the body to facilitate the movement of one tissue over another – most commonly muscle and tendinous structures moving over bony surfaces. The quantity of fluid they contain is minute and it is almost impossible to locate or retrieve fluid from a normal bursa.

Bursae are found under the muscles at the point of the shoulder (the bicipital bursa) to ease the movement of the biceps muscle over the shoulder joint. Another very important bursa is located between the navicular bone (navicular bursa) and the deep digital flexor tendon, which passes over it on the way to its attachment on the sole of the pedal bone (see page 133). Another bursa lies between the bony point of the hock and the gastrocnemius tendon that passes over it (the calcancal bursa).

Bursitis

Inflammation is termed bursitis and is usually the result of trauma: either blunt trauma, such as a blow, or a fall or traumatic strain caused by overuse. The result of this is an increase in fluid content and a thickening of the sac wall. Rest and treatment at this stage will often restore the bursa to its normal size. Repeated trauma can cause permanent enlargement and thickening, where the sac wall develops scar tissue that cannot be reduced.

Lameness may occur in both acute and chronic bursitis, and may be the result of severe inflammation and excess fluid causing painful distension of the sac. Inflammation of the lining that secretes the fluid can also contribute to the pain. When such tissues are irritated their normal function goes into overdrive and produces excess fluid.

Early treatment is advisable because the wall of the bursa contains elastic fibres that lose their elasticity if chronically over-stretched and are then unable to return to their original shape.

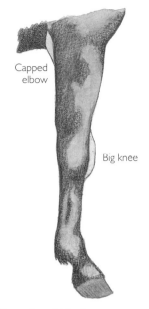
Examples of false bursae.

False bursae

True bursae are often quite deep and cannot easily be found. The soft swellings that many owners will have experienced are false bursae. These are fluid-filled sacs that develop just under the skin over bony prominences, such as the elbow and hock. They are usually only subcutaneous (under the skin) and resemble, in structure and content, the blisters that we might acquire after too much yard sweeping.

False bursae are most likely to be caused by repeated, external trauma, such as the horse lying on a bare floor. Typical examples are capped hocks, capped elbows and big knees. Repeated injury causes superficial layers of tissue to tear and fill with fluid. This fluid is derived from serum that seeps into the space between the torn tissues.

False bursae do not have a natural retaining sac membrane and can therefore spread if the trauma is not prevented. With time, however, scar tissue will form in the damaged tissue and encapsulate the fluid. These chronic false bursae are also called hygromas. The most common one occurs on the front of the knee as a result of the horse banging his stable door or hitting fences when jumping.

Bursal enlargement of the knee is often caused by door banging.

Emergency: risk of infection

In severe cases of soft fluid swellings, it may be necessary to drain the structure and inject a corticosteroid directly into the space. This must be performed under strict aseptic conditions (free from the risk of infection). Infection in any synovial structure is potentially catastrophic and must be avoided at all costs. Penetrating injuries in and around a synovial bursa or sheath frequently result in infection. This must be treated very urgently by flushing, usually with the horse under general anaesthesia.

Infection usually manifests itself as a severe lameness with very rapid onset.

Such injuries are surprisingly common during hunting or cross-country jumping, when even minor wounds might puncture a synovial structure. Rapid veterinary attention usually results in full resolution, but these injuries must be recognized as a true emergency for treatment to be fully effective.

Both true bursae and tendon sheaths have a synovial membrane lining. This lining secretes synovial fluid in a similar way to the synovial membrane lining in a joint capsule. False bursae, or hygromas, have no specific lining. Their fluid is derived from tissue fluid and serum leaking into the tissue space, and is much less viscous (thick and sticky) than synovial fluid.

Fetlocks and hocks

Windgalls are fluid enlargements that are similar in function to bursae. However, they are really enlargements of the tendon sheath as it passes through the canal at the back of the fetlock.

If windgalls occur at the fetlock they are correctly referred to as tendinous or non-articular windgalls. If the fetlock joint capsule itself is enlarged, this is referred to as an articular windgall. Distinguishing one from the other can be difficult for owners as the two windgalls lie side by side.

Causes range from tenosynovitis (an inflammation of the lining of the sheath) to damage of the superficial or deep flexor tendon. Swelling could also be due to annular ligament syndrome – this is a restriction at the back of the fetlock that often causes lameness. These latter problems can be diagnosed by a vet using ultrasonography and diagnostic analgesia (where a local anaesthetic is used).

Another common tendon sheath enlargement is the thoroughpin, which is found in the top of the hock under the tendons just above the point of the hock. This is the tendon sheath of the deep digital flexor tendon. In bog spavin the swelling is sited high on the outside and low on the inside of the hock.

Treatment

Correct treatment for all these problems is important, and urgent, if the swellings are to be reduced. They are unlikely to result in lameness, but are of cosmetic significance which many owners find unacceptable.

The swelling of either true bursae or tendon sheaths is an

indication of injury to the structure they are designed to protect. Lameness is less likely in the early stages but, when lameness is present, veterinary advice is necessary.

Effective treatment for any of the injuries mentioned here depends on early recognition and prevention of the cause, be it overwork or superficial trauma, if repeated injury is to be prevented. Rest and possibly even immobilization of the area, with support bandaging, is also often very beneficial. As with any inflammatory condition, cold therapy will reduce the blood flow and secretion of excess fluid into the sacs or the torn tissue spaces.

Your vet may choose to treat the tendon sheath with anti-inflammatory drugs, such as cortisone, perhaps used in

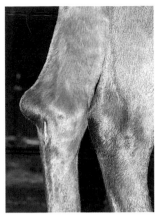

Capped hocks can be a result of the horse lying on a bare floor.

Case study: Possible diagnoses

My horse has soft, fluid-like swellings on her hocks that do not appear to cause her any pain. What are they?

Check your horse's legs every day for any swollen areas.

Swellings in the hock region are common in horses of all ages and breeds. The fact that the swellings you describe are present on both hocks, are soft and appear to be fluid-filled excludes some conditions such as degenerative joint disease of the hock. However, presuming your horse is not lame, this still leaves a number of possible diagnoses.

The location of the swelling in relation to the different anatomical structures of the hock will allow your vet to obtain a diagnosis but, in general, swellings around the front of the hock would suggest distension of the tarsocrural (largest) hock joint. This may be due to inflammation of the joint as a result of trauma or could be secondary to a fragment of bone floating within the joint. If there is a fragment of bone, it could be related to trauma or a condition called osteochondritis dissecans (OCD). This is a condition seen in many horses, most often Warmbloods, where inflammation of the joint arises from a defect in the development of bone and cartilage. X-rays could confirm or exclude these possibilities and surgery may be required to assess and treat some of these conditions.

Swellings in other areas of the hock are also quite common. Capped hocks are swellings at the point of the hock and are usually of cosmetic importance only, as are thoroughpins.

Curbs are generally firm swellings at the back of the hock and ultrasonography may be necessary to examine these, so speak to your vet about this.

conjunction with hyaluronic acid – a natural product within all joints and tendon sheaths.

Eventually, all the swellings described will become cold and pain-free – they may even disappear completely. The aim of treatment is to reduce them as far as possible and avoid an ugly lump. However, it must be noted that these swellings are markers for injury and strain to deeper tendinous structures – which is why early recognition and rest are so important.

Purpura

Purpura is a condition classified as an auto-immune disease. An event triggers the immune system to begin to attack the horse's body, and in the case of purpura the target tissue is the blood vessels. The defence system destroys the walls of the vessels, making them leaky and unable to carry blood. The main trigger event for this abnormal defence activity is infection by bacteria called *Streptococci* (the same bacteria that cause strangles).

Signs of purpura include swelling in the legs, patches of swollen tissue along the body, tiredness, a high temperature, and small haemorrhages visible on the membranes of the mouth and genitalia.

The leg swelling can become large and interfere with blood flow to the feet. Permanent blood vessel damage can also lead to the drainage in the leg becoming less efficient, which in turn may lead to laminitis. Damage to the blood vessels can remain even after treatment, which is aimed at suppressing the defence system with corticosteroids.

Splints

Horses have several anatomical features that are evolutionary remnants of functional structures in their ancestors. Sometimes these structures – such as the chestnut – are accepted as normal anatomy in the modern horse and cause no problem.

Another evolutionary remnant that has lost some, but not all, of its function is the splint bone. This is the much-reduced remnant of what was once the equivalent of a cannon bone. A splint bone is found lying slightly behind and on either side of every cannon bone, so there are two on each limb. When the splint was a functional cannon bone, the horse had three digits and three hooves on each leg. This was about 50 million years ago, when the horse was about the size of a small deer.

Function and form

Unlike the chestnuts, the splint bones (more correctly named metacarpal bones on the forelegs and metatarsal bones on the hindlegs) have not lost all function, and this is one of the reasons that they occasionally cause problems.

The splint bones are fine and delicate for most of their length, but the head of each bone is quite large and forms part of the lower articular surface of the knee or hock. From the head, the bone tapers very quickly to a thin shaft only a few millimetres in diameter. The whole bone finishes about three-quarters of the way down the cannon bone as a small, roundish swelling known as the button of the splint. The shaft and the button can be identified easily by careful palpation of the limb.

Splint bones are unusual in being in contact with another bone at one end only. The inside (medial) splint bone is usually larger than the outside (lateral) bone, and this is a source of one of the problems we associate with these bones.

To avoid confusion, it is sensible to refer to the bones by their correct anatomical names, as most horse owners understand the term 'splint' to mean the hard, bony swelling found along the cannon bone that often causes lameness. So from now on we will refer to these abnormal swellings as splints and to the normal bones as metacarpals or metatarsals.

The cannon bone is either a metacarpal or a metatarsal bone, so the bones are all given numbers for descriptive simplification, each with an appropriate abbreviation. For example, the cannon bone is the third metacarpal or metatarsal bone (Mc_{III} or Mt_{III}), the inside bone is the second (Mc_{II} or Mt_{II}) and the outside bone the fourth (Mc_{IV} or Mt_{IV})

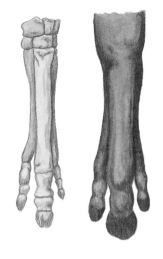

Millions of years ago, the horse had limbs with three digits (hooves). Remnants of these can be seen in the splint bones lying to either side and slightly below the cannon bone in today's horses.

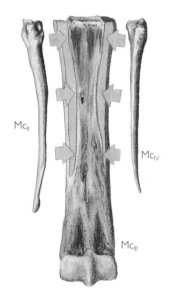

Mc_{II}

Mc_{IV}

Mc_{III}

Metacarpal (cannon and splint) bones in the horse's foreleg.

Some splints are immediately obvious without palpation.

Right leg
(rotated view)

Right leg
(from behind)

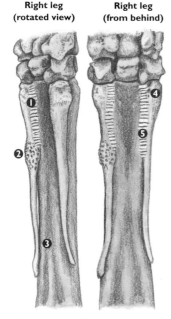

❶ Interosseus ligament
❷ Splint on medial (inside) metacarpal bone (Mc$_{II}$)
❸ Cannon bone (Mc$_{III}$)
❹ Lateral (outside) metacarpal bone (Mc$_{IV}$)
❺ Interosseus ligament

Where to look

Splints can occur at almost any site along the inside or outside of the cannon bones. They can be small and detected only by careful palpation, or they can be so large that they are immediately obvious. Equally, they can be pain-free and of cosmetic significance only, or they can be quite painful and cause pronounced lameness. Size does not necessarily indicate a painful growth: some large splints can cause no pain while some small splints can make a horse lame for weeks.

The most common site for splints is along the inside of the cannon bone and particularly on the forelimb. The reason for this is that the medial (inside) metacarpal bone bears weight from the above row of carpal bones, but the bone that sits on the head of the lateral (outside) splint bone also sits on the cannon bone. This means that the inside metacarpal is subjected to more downward pressure than the outside bone, although they both move down and up slightly during weight-bearing and non-weight-bearing movement. As the forelimbs bear more weight than the hindlimbs, the predisposition to splint formation is greater on the forelimbs.

Splint formation

Between the metacarpal/metatarsal bones and the cannon bone is a strong ligament called the interosseous ligament that binds the two together. Tearing of this ligament causes pain and swelling, and is the primary source of a splint:

- If the tear is mild and no palpable swelling can be detected, the lameness is often referred to as a blind splint.
- A large or obvious splint may be termed a true splint.
- Multiple bony lumps along the cannon bone may be referred to as chain splints.

The initial swelling, which can be as large as a hen's egg, is composed of soft tissue and oedema (fluid), although it may feel quite hard to the touch. It will often appear very quickly over one or two days and in some cases will reduce equally quickly after a week or two before it has time to convert to bone. In other cases, the swelling calcifies and the horse is left with a hard, bony lump that may remain for the rest of his life. Occasionally, the lump will reduce over two to three years to become insignificant. Almost any combination of size, lameness, growth rate or regression can occur in splints, which can be a law unto themselves.

Preventing splints

It is difficult to prevent a horse developing splints but, remembering the cause (see above), we can help by reducing concussion. Too much work on hard surfaces, particularly when the horse is young and physically immature, will increase concussion and predispose the animal to splint formation. Young horses galloping loose in the paddock on hard summer ground and too much trotting on the road all increase the risk. Splints can also be formed if the area is knocked by accident.

The best way to avoid splints is to be careful about the amount of hard work you give a young horse. Similarly, protecting lower limbs against the traumatic effect of striking the opposite limb with a shoe when turning sharply, particularly when unbalanced, will also help.

Treatment

A variety of remedies can be used to help reduce the swelling and pain or lameness. These are combinations of anti-inflammatory treatments such as cold bandaging, bute or injection of corticosteroids while the splint is relatively soft.

Rest will reduce the movement of the metacarpal/metatarsal bones and tearing of the interosseous ligament, and is a useful part of treatment if lameness is present. Ensuring that the feet are balanced and weight distribution is even across the limb can help in many cases.

After a short period, usually a few weeks, these soft lumps will harden as they calcify and turn to bone. Once this has occurred splints are often more difficult to treat, as the bony lump has

Conformation problems

Splints are more likely to occur if the horse has poor leg conformation. Angular limb deformities through the knee can increase the pressure down the side of the cannon bone, particularly if the limb deviates outwards, and deprive the inside of the limb of adequate support by the hoof. This uneven weight distribution across the base of the knee will also encourage splint formation. It is also thought by some that horses with a short, heavy stride are more prone to developing splints than horses with a longer action and lighter footfall.

to alter in order to reduce in size. This natural process can take weeks or even months. Treatment is aimed at trying to speed up this process by increasing the blood flow to the splint by using mild blisters. You should ask your vet which splint remedy he would prescribe.

Problem patients

Once the initial reaction has resolved and settled down, splints rarely cause problems to horses – but there are exceptions.

Behind the bone

If the splint (which is actually bony callus) is large and grows behind the cannon bone rather than outwards from the cannon, it can rub on the tendons or suspensory ligament and cause lameness. In such cases it is necessary to remove the splint surgically and restore the bone to its normal profile.

Cosmetic

In show horses and ponies, the cosmetic appearance of the limbs is crucial and the presence of even a small splint can mar a show career, so splints are often removed. Removal for any reason is not without risk because the process itself, which involves using chisels and mallets, is traumatic and can lead to the formation of another splint at the site of removal. Once settled and pain-free, however, it is rarely necessary to remove splints from the majority of horses.

Trauma fracture

Another injury commonly encountered is a broken metacarpal or metatarsal bone following a kick by another horse or trauma from a jump or fall. Fractures occur quite commonly in polo ponies after the bone has been struck by a ball or mallet. A fracture usually results in a significant callus but it will eventually settle down in the same way that a true splint does. If the fracture does not stabilize, the fractured end is usually easily removed and the horse restored to soundness.

Ringbone

Ringbone is so called because horses suffering from it develop a bony enlargement which, in severe cases, can ring the pastern. People talk about high and low ringbone: this refers to the joints that are affected, namely, the pastern joint and coffin joint respectively.

Ringbone is caused by trauma or tearing of the periosteum and is common in heavy horses with heavy action. Articular ringbone encroaches into the joint and a horse with this condition is therefore unlikely to become sound; however, non-articular ringbone does not involve the joint and the horse is more likely to return to soundness.

Ligament injuries to the joint are common. The pastern and coffin joints have two major ligaments, one on each side of the joint as you look from the front, called the collateral ligaments. Damage to one or both of these can dramatically affect joint stability. If the joint is unstable or loose, the body produces extra new bone around the edges of the joint. Unfortunately, the effect of this is to reduce joint mobility and make movement painful.

In very rare cases, this process will eventually lead to fusion of the joint – the ultimate in stability. Once there is no more movement in the joint, there is no more pain. This is similar to the process that goes on in spavin (see pages 128–129), where the small joints at the base of the hock degenerate and cause pain, but eventually fuse and from then on the horse tends to be sound. The unfortunate thing with ringbone is that fusion of the coffin joint is complicated by the presence of the navicular bone, and the pastern joint is a relatively high-motion joint.

X-rays will establish how severe the degenerative process is and which joint, or joints, are affected. The vet will then have a much better picture of how the horse is likely to perform. Treatment may vary from box rest to – in the most serious cases – having the horse put down.

If the pastern joint is affected, surgical fusion can be attempted, but this is not cheap and there are considerable risks. Surgical

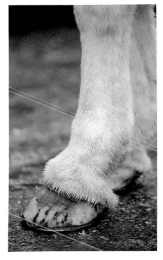

Bony enlargement typical of low ringbone.

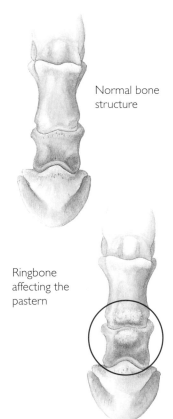

Normal bone structure

Ringbone affecting the pastern

fusion of the coffin joint is not possible. In milder cases, injections of steroids with or without additional hyaluronic acid preparations can be useful in improving clinical signs, but do little for the underlying cause.

Sidebone

There are many reasons why a horse contracts sidebone. One of these factors is poor shoeing; others include poor conformation and excessive concussion. These factors generally cause excessive trauma to the hoof, in turn causing ossification (hardening) of one or both of the lateral cartilages – these are attached to either side of the pedal bone and extend above the coronet. When this happens it may cause no problem at all, or it may interfere with the way the soft tissues around the area stretch and adjust during exercise. This can cause pain and discomfort, although most cases of sidebone do not result in pain.

Generally, once the sidebone has hardened the horse should become sound. Until then, the sidebone-affected foot ideally should be shod to the wear pattern of the shoe that has been taken off.

Sidebone – affects one or both of the lateral cartilages.

Bone chips

Complex injuries can occur in joints when fragments of bone are detached in an accident. The joint will remain painful unless the fragment is minute.

Small fragments of bone in a joint are a common finding but, reassuringly, they cause little problem. They are most likely to appear on the margins of the articular surface, and occur if the joint capsule has been torn from its attachment to the bone – in the process, a fragment of bone is often pulled away from the parent bone. Excessive, abnormal movement can cause pieces of bone to detach in a nutcracker-like action. This injury would most commonly be found in the knees of young racehorses.

Contrary to common belief, joint fragments (unless quite

large) are very rarely detached and loose in the joint. Most chips retain some attachment to the joint capsule or to neighbouring articular cartilage, which prevents them from floating about in the joint.

Removal of such chips is by arthroscopy (keyhole surgery). The decision to operate will be based on the size of the fragment and whether it is causing a major problem to the horse.

Small joint fragments, sometimes referred to as joint mice, are a common finding on routine X-rays and do not indicate a serious problem. They simply suggest that, at some time in the past, the joint suffered an injury.

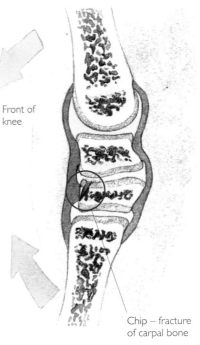

Front of knee

Chip – fracture of carpal bone

Pedal bone fractures

Fractures of the pedal bone vary in their seriousness, depending on where the fracture is located in the bone. A fracture at the very end of the wing of the pedal bone will not involve the joint. Therefore, it will have a much better outlook compared to a fracture into the joint. The hoof wall acts as a natural cast to the fractured pedal bone and, in order to further strengthen this protection, a round shoe can be fitted. This shoe will counter any slight movement of the foot when weight bearing (ask your vet and farrier for advice on this). The fracture will eventually heal enough to allow athletic activity, but will be visible on X-rays for a long time afterwards.

The total time needed off work in order for the fracture to heal will vary from four to six months. The point at which the horse can return to work will depend on when he stops exhibiting pain at the trot and when pain on application of hoof testers disappears. Your vet is the best person to make these judgements, and he will also be able to advise on turnout, leading in-hand, and finally a gradually increasing programme of ridden exercise. Provided the final radiographs are satisfactory and there is no evidence of any coffin joint osteoarthritis, there is no reason why the horse cannot return to the work he was doing before the fracture.

Hyper-extension of the knee, for example during fast work, creates a nutcracker-like action which may cause disruption of the bone at the front of the joint. Small fragments of bone may not result in lameness if the 'chip' remains attached to the joint capsule (as shown).

Boxy feet

'Boxy feet' are more upright than normal hooves: the latter should have a hoof wall that is parallel to the hoof-pastern axis and the angle of the heels (see diagram bottom left on page 177). Boxy feet are more common in some breeds than others, but where one hoof is becoming more boxy than the other, it is a cause for concern. In many cases, a boxy foot may indicate that there is a degree of heel pain, even if there is no lameness at this stage. The horse may be adapting to heel pain by loading the toe and not the heel.

Get your vet to examine your horse and X-ray both forefeet. If there are indicators of heel pain, treatment can begin before the horse becomes lame. This is a situation where your vet and farrier can work together to prevent the problem developing further.

Poor feet

Poor hoof horn generally manifests itself as hoof cracks, brittle feet, thin soles that are prone to bruising and/or collapsed heels. There are several ways in which you can improve horn quality.

Diet

Ensure that you are feeding your horse a balanced diet. Horses and ponies often have unique requirements for certain nutrients to help improve the condition of their feet, and research has shown that some horses benefit from specific supplementation. It is important to appreciate that the best results in improved horn growth and condition require a combination of these nutrients, rather than supplementing just one.

The composition of the hoof wall means the horse must have an adequate supply of essential amino acids. Diets that are deficient in quality protein can lead to reduced hoof growth, splitting and cracking. Alfalfa is a good source of quality protein and contains good levels of essential amino acids, as well as calcium and magnesium. You can feed up to 1.5kg (3¼lb) per day.

Alternatively, if your horse is a good doer, consider using a low-calorie feed balancer. These contain quality protein sources and higher levels of trace elements, but are low in calories. They need only be fed in small amounts on a daily basis and can be mixed with a handful of chaff or alfalfa to encourage chewing.

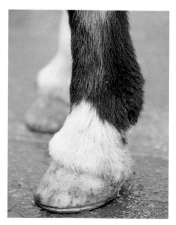

Special hoof supplements will provide the nutrients required to enhance hoof growth and improve the strength of the horn. Biotin has been reported to increase the rate of horn growth and improve hardness in the horn at the toe and quarters. Methionine also helps to promote rapid horn growth.

Specially formulated hoof supplements can help to improve the quality of a horse's feet.

Some hoof supplements contain yeast culture to increase nutrient digestibility, mineral absorption and protein utilization.

Environment

Good quality horn can withstand most of the environmental challenges that domesticated horses are likely to encounter. However, poor quality horn is susceptible to a variety of problems caused by its inability to regulate moisture content in the foot. Wet horn is weaker than dry horn and is prone to bacterial invasion, so if your horse's feet are poor it is advisable to avoid situations where bacteria can thrive. This means keeping his bedding clean and

Poor hoof quality can be improved through diet, but it will take a long time.

Case study: Going barefoot

I have a four-year-old cob cross who has been lightly backed. He has his hooves trimmed regularly, but has never had metal shoes fitted. I'd like to keep him barefoot as I feel it's more natural. However, as I want to bring him on this year, and hack out on forest tracks, I appreciate he may need extra protection. What should I do?

There are many new types of shoe, and shoeing methods, available and they all have their place for certain types of horses in a variety of circumstances. Horses' feet vary greatly in shape and form, and what works for one won't necessarily work for another.

Your farrier is the person to ask for advice on this. He will know your horse's feet and will recognize any changes in them when your youngster starts to be ridden out. You may find that your horse can cope with light work on the forest tracks with no shoes at all. You will soon be able

to tell if he feels footsore, and your farrier will recognize any extra hoof wear. If there are any problems, it may be that conventional shoes, hoof boots or some other form of 'shoes' are necessary – again, your farrier will be able to advise you.

It is always commendable when owners want to keep their horses in a manner that is as close to their natural lifestyle as possible. It is important, though, to bear in mind that we often ask far more of them than they would ever do in the wild, and so we have to make sure we adjust our care accordingly.

Pigeon toes

Pigeon toes are a conformation fault in which the toes point inwards, with the deviation usually starting from the fetlocks down. This type of conformation is very common and, provided it isn't exaggerated, should not pose any problems.

Pigeon toes cause the horse to dish in trot. Very exaggerated pigeon toes can lead to fetlock and pastern joint problems because of the uneven pressure on them.

One problem can be fetlock joint effusion. This is where extra fluid builds up on the joint. It can be diagnosed by the appearance of pouches of fluid just behind the cannon bone, near the fetlock.

This fluid indicates that the joint is aggravated, either by a recent trauma or, if present for a longer period of time, possibly an arthritic problem. Signs of pain may accompany this fluid when the joint is flexed, and the horse can become lame.

If you are worried that your horse's pigeon toes are severe enough to cause problems contact your vet, who will be able to tell you what action needs to be taken, if any.

dry, and trying to avoid him standing for long periods in wet, muddy fields. (For more detail on stabilizing moisture content in the foot, see pages 39–40.)

Farriery

Poor quality horn also means that the horse may be prone to losing shoes, especially in summer when the dry weather and hard ground can cause splits and cracks. Repetitive nailing into the same area can weaken feet, but it is sometimes necessary in order to hold shoes on. A temporary option is to glue shoes on as this is less risky than hot shoeing and/or nailing. Provide your farrier with a clean and dry

Hot shoeing may not be the best option for horses with weak feet.

shoeing area to give him the best chance to get the glue to stick. You should also be careful not to allow the shoes to be pulled, so use overreach boots. Removing shoes for eight weeks in the autumn gives the feet time to recover before re-shoeing.

With correct farriery, a well-balanced diet and good management, your horse should grow better feet. However, it does take a long time: the hoof grows from the coronet band and it takes up to a year for the improved quality horn to grow to where it hits the ground.

Corns

Corns occur in the part of the sole called (unsurprisingly) the seat of corn – that is, at the angle of the heel. A corn is an area of bruised sole that swells as it absorbs fluid from the bruising and causes localized pressure and pain. The most usual cause is ill-fitting shoes (often due to their having been left on too long) that put pressure on the sole, or sometimes a stone or something similar trapped between the shoe and the sole.

A horse that is suffering from a corn or corns will be lame, although this may be intermittent. Diagnosis can be made using hoof testers to locate the pain and paring away the sole to reveal the bruising, which shows as reddish (blood-stained) horn.

The shoe must be removed and the corn trimmed out. A special shoe can be applied to avoid putting pressure on the area. If the area is infected, poulticing may be required (see overleaf).

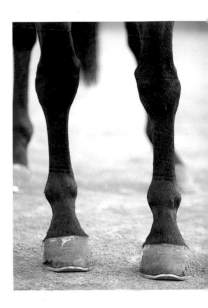

Bruised sole

Riding over rough ground is the classic cause of a bruised sole and occurs more frequently in flat-footed horses (notably Thoroughbred types). The horse will be moderately to severely lame, and this is usually noticed a few hours after the initial bruising occurred. Hoof testers will reveal the area of pain, which will become discoloured over a period of time as blood gradually leaks into the sole.

Rest is the primary treatment, along with protection of the sole if necessary. The bruising will usually resolve within a week or two and the horse will become sound again.

Punctured sole

A punctured sole is usually caused by the horse stepping on a nail, shard of glass or sharp stone, which may still be embedded in the sole but is sometimes difficult to see. Because the entry hole is small (allowing for little drainage) and the wound often deep, it frequently becomes infected and the horse will suddenly become acutely lame due to pressure from the pus.

These wounds can be serious so call your vet, who will clean and perhaps pare the sole of the foot to reveal a black area that marks the entry spot. If the area is pressed, pus may ooze.

Your vet will cut away the horn to allow the wound to drain properly. The foot should then be poulticed (see overleaf) until no more pus is evident, when the hole can be plugged to prevent any debris entering the wound

Poulticing

There are two kinds of poultice: hot and cold. Cold poultices are used to reduce swelling around bruised areas; hot poultices apply damp heat to draw out an infection.

There are many ready-made poultices on the market that are quick to use, clean and do not interfere with the wound. They can usually be used for both hot and cold treatments.

You will need:

- Poultice
- Scissors
- Hot water (for hot poultice)
- Plastic bag
- Cotton wool
- Adhesive bandage

Foot abscess

An abscess, or 'pus in the foot', is caused by infection developing perhaps following a penetrating wound, bruised foot or corn. Infection may also enter via a white line that has become stretched and weakened due to poor or irregular shoeing and/or trimming. It will generally cause severe lameness in which the horse is very reluctant to place any weight on the infected foot. As with any abscess, prompt evacuation of the pus will hasten recovery.

Foot abscesses should be poulticed and drained, and this involves careful paring of the sole of the foot by a vet or experienced farrier to release the infection. If the infection is not released and is allowed to fester, it will create more damage until it eventually bursts out at the heels or coronary band. Make sure the horse is up to date with his tetanus protection. Antibiotics are not recommended as they may suppress the infection, and are certainly no substitute for careful examination with a hoof knife.

I Clean the underside of the foot thoroughly, as the sole of the foot must come into contact with the poultice. Cut the poultice to a size that will cover the affected area. It is better too big than too small.

If you want a hot poultice, put it into water as hot as you can bear. Otherwise, follow the manufacturer's soaking instructions. Wring out the poultice until it stops dripping.

Press the poultice over the damaged area (medicated side next to the foot) and cover it with a plastic bag.

2 Place a thick layer of cotton wool over the plastic.

3 Bandage over the poultice to secure it and keep the heat in. Replace the poultice every 12 hours.

4 Finished poultice viewed from the underside of the hoof.

White line disease

White line disease is quite a common problem, varying in degrees of severity. If the area becomes infected, generally only in severe cases, lameness can be evident.

White line disease is caused by the horny and sensitive laminae pulling apart. This leaves gaps, which then allow dirt and grit to penetrate into the sensitive hoof. This in turn creates a cavity that rots and causes the breakdown of the laminae.

Laminitis is a very common cause as it does dramatic damage to the laminae, leaving them wide open to infiltrating foreign bodies. Contact your vet if your horse is lame, as there is a very good chance infection is present and antibiotics may be required.

The bacteria involved in white line disease are anaerobic, which means they live without oxygen. Because of this, an effective solution is to open the cavity to the air. Once the area is clean, your farrier will probably want to treat it with an acrylic or antibacterial putty to prevent re-infection.

After this, you should make sure your horse's feet are shod or trimmed regularly, to nip any potential problems in the bud before they develop. Correct basic hoof care should also be exercised. This includes picking out feet daily and keeping them as clean as possible.

Good basic hoof care, including picking out your horse's feet daily, is important in both treating and preventing white line disease.

Thrush

Thrush is an infection of the frog of the horse's foot, often brought about by poor foot care and unhygienic practices in the stable. Dirt and faecal material can easily be trapped in the crevices on either side of the frog. If this is not cleaned out it provides a wonderful moisture-rich environment for the bacteria that cause thrush to thrive.

These bacteria eat into the frog tissue, creating a fetid grey-to-black liquid that has a very characteristic smell – once smelt, never forgotten! In addition, the frog starts to fall apart. This can cause some discomfort to the horse, but rarely outright

Regular soaking in antifungal agents can help to beat thrush.

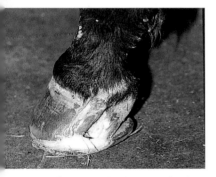

Crack that has been cut back.

Repair to a crack, with the two sides screwed together.

lameness unless it is left to penetrate the underlying soft, sensitive tissue of the foot.

Prevention is better than cure. Good practices include care over hygiene, daily picking out of the feet, regular and accurate hoof trimming, and turnout on dry pasture.

Treatment involves the removal of the affected parts of the frog using a hoof knife (this must be done by a vet or farrier). Then antibiotic spray, iodine solution or a 10% formaldehyde solution can be applied to the infected areas. Healing time is generally short (10–14 days) because the infection is usually only shallow and does not affect the deeper layers of the foot.

If the deep tissues of the foot have been affected, local anaesthesia or sedation of the horse may be needed to allow your vet to operate and remove the infection. Afterwards, the foot may need to be bandaged with iodine-soaked swabs for a few days until healthy new frog tissue re-forms. Daily foot soaking in antifungal agents may be recommended and, most importantly, the horse should be kept in the driest conditions possible. If large amounts of hoof wall have been removed, an acrylic can be used to fill in the defect once the infection has been eliminated. However, this process can take weeks, running to several months, until the infection has been completely resolved.

Hoof cracks

Hoof wall cracks are a common problem and range from shallow lines in the surface to deep fissures that extend to the sensitive layers of the foot and cause pain.

The cause is usually abnormal mechanical forces acting on a weak or unbalanced hoof capsule. Injuries to the capsule will also give rise to cracks, which can start at the ground surface or the coronet. Unshod horses in the field are most vulnerable, so it is vital your farrier trims your horse's feet regularly to remove excess growth.

Most moderate cracks, known as sandcracks, are best treated by good balancing and trimming by the farrier, and placing additional clips on the shoes on each side of the crack to prevent it extending. If the foot is left too long, leverage will be exerted differently on the two sides of the crack and this then requires urgent specialist treatment.

The first task in such cases is to explore the crack and open it up to its full limits. It will often be underrun for some distance on either side of the crack with soft, crumbly horn. This must be cut back to normal horn to remove any unhealthy or infected tissue. The sides of the crack must be stabilized by the use of a bar shoe and extra clips and, in some cases, wiring or screwing the two sides together to prevent movement.

If the crack has not reached the coronet, it is important to prevent it doing so. This is achieved by cutting a deep horizontal groove in the horn which then acts like a moat. This allows the outer capsule to flex below the groove, but the crack cannot extend across the moat because there is no contact between the two sides. The recovery time for such injuries will depend on the degree of lameness and the extent of the defect, but is usually several months.

Seedy toe

A similar condition to hoof cracks, seedy toe is essentially the same as white line disease. In this case, the white line (where the sole of the foot joins the hoof wall), usually in the toe region, becomes infected with bacteria and fungi. It then deteriorates into a soft, crumbly texture. This can be caused by the toe getting too long, excess burning by a hot shoe during shoeing, or by stones being driven into the horn.

The most common incidence, however, is in cases of chronic laminitis where separation of the hoof has occurred through the white line. The only way to solve the problem is to remove the defective horn back to normal tissue. This is achieved by opening up and removing the overlying wall. Seedy toe rarely causes lameness in the early stages, but it does cause separation of areas of the capsule from the inner layers of the hoof. Ultimately, this will affect hoof strength, soundness and shoe retention.

Using synthetics

In both seedy toe and wall crack problems, the defect created by curetting (scraping) away the horn may be repaired with modern synthetic materials. However, this may not always be desirable, or necessary. The gap between the hoof and the repair material may harbour contaminants, which can become trapped and introduce new infection. If it is possible to leave the defect open, this will ensure that thorough cleaning is possible.

This hoof shows symptoms of seedy toe.

Seedy toe after the affected horn has been cut away.

Shoeing alternatives

As veterinary science advances, and our understanding of horses' needs improves, new ideas on all aspects of horse care constantly appear. Farriery is no exception. Several new schools of thought claim to have found more sympathetic ways to shoe – methods that reflect the way horses' feet were naturally intended to be.

The trouble with hooves

The equine foot is a complex structure. The hoof and the bones inside it are under constant pressure and can easily go wrong. Some horses are born with poor feet but many of the defects we see develop over time and can be a reflection of the way the horse has been trimmed and shod.

A good relationship between a competent farrier and a knowledgeable owner makes all the difference to the horse. It is down to you to gain sufficient knowledge of horses' feet to allow you to spot potential problems.

Farriery is a skilful job but, in reality, the standard of shoeing varies greatly. Incorrect farriery is a recognized cause of serious problems such as navicular, and owners must be selective about who they trust with their horse's feet. Saving money by choosing the cheapest farrier could leave you facing a large vet's bill at the end of the day.

Getting the balance right

Techniques such as Natural Balance and Cytek shoeing are based on achieving what they believe is the ideal foot balance. A properly balanced foot is the right shape and strength to support the horse's body. It also allows him to move in the best possible way.

Foot balance

The traditional approach to foot balance involves looking at the horse's feet while they are on the ground. Bone and limb alignment is easy to see on a clean, level surface and it is important that owners are aware of it. Basically, from the side, you are looking for a good hoof-pastern angle.

From the back you should see a foot that is standing squarely with the weight evenly distributed on both sides.

Always talk to your farrier if you are worried about your horse. The farrier only sees your horse for about an hour every six weeks, you see him every day. The owner is the expert: you know more about your horse than anyone. If you don't think your horse is right, your farrier should listen to your concerns.

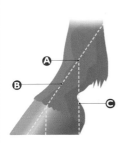

Broken-line hoof-pastern axis
The hoof to pastern line is not straight. This is known as a broken-back hoof-pastern axis and shows that the bones of the foot are not correctly aligned.

Straight-line hoof-pastern axis
Begin by standing the horse squarely on level ground. Find the centre of rotation of the fetlock joint by running your hand down the sides of the leg over the widest part of the cannon bone until you touch the fetlock joint (Ⓐ). Imagine a line passing through the centre of all the joints below this point to the ground. This line from hoof to pastern (Ⓑ) should be straight and the line from the fetlock joint to the ground (Ⓒ) should meet the last weight-bearing part of the heel.

Rear view
The foot should look symmetrical from behind.

When the feet are not in balance, the horse's natural movement is altered. This puts stress and strain on the structures of his feet, legs and body. Common problems that can arise as a result include navicular, arthritis, stumbling and back problems.

Nature's way

In the wild, horses exist without the need for farriers. Wild horses balance their own feet by wearing them down in a way that best suits their conformation and movement. Domestic horses are not able to do this. In the wild, horses seem to survive very well on their own and hardly ever suffer from foot trouble, even though they are constantly on the move and often crossing rough ground. This has prompted researchers to compare wild horses' feet to those of domestic horses, who tend to be plagued with so many foot and lameness problems.

Studies of wild horses' feet have sparked new thinking on the way domestic horses should be shod. Natural Balance and

This young dressage horse competes barefoot. His feet are trimmed using the Natural Balance method.

Cytek shoeing are based on research carried out with wild horses. Advocates of these methods believe that, although their lives are very different, the needs of horses' feet are always the same whether they are wild or domesticated and working.

The main argument against shoeing methods based on wild horse studies is precisely the opposite of this: that you cannot apply observations of feral horses' feet living in particular locations and conditions to every horse, domesticated or wild. Various shoeing methods may be appropriate for different horses in varying situations – you cannot apply one method to all horses in all situations.

Natural Balance

According to its originator, Gene Ovnicek, Natural Balance is 'a combination of simple guidelines which address the basic needs of the equine foot, whether it's wild, domestic, shod or barefoot. These are determined from scientific research, common sense, biomechanics and practical experience.'

In studying wild horses and developing Natural Balance, Gene found a way to identify distortions of the foot. Although he agrees that looking at the hoof-pastern axis (see page 177) is a good guide, he thinks more can be learned about the state of the foot and the bones inside it by examining its underside.

One of the most important features of Natural Balance is the assessment of the foot, and horse owners themselves can do this. First draw a line across the widest part of the foot with a marker pen. Then draw a line across the back part of the heel and look at the spaces between. The rear portion should ideally cover two-thirds of the foot. If the front part covers anything more than one-third it's a warning sign of foot distortion.

A balanced view

Natural Balance is a way of trimming and shoeing that mimics the naturally balanced feet Gene saw in wild horses. Its belief is that equines are designed to bear weight with the frog, bars and sole (in contrast to more traditional shoeing, where much

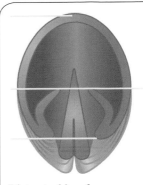

Distorted hoof
- There is more foot ahead of the widest point.
- The toe area is oval in shape.
- The heel is under the foot and well ahead of the back of the frog.
- The heel bulbs have become pointed.
- The frog is narrow and pointed, and the central groove is deep and narrow.
- The bars curve sharply.

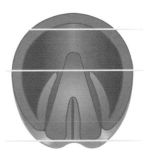

Normal hoof
- There is more foot behind the widest point.
- The toe area is well rounded.
- The heel is wide and close to the back part of the frog, and the heel bulbs are wide and rounded.
- The frog is wide and rounded, and the central groove is wide and shallow.
- The bars curve subtly.

Natural Balance shoes are a very different shape to traditional shoes.

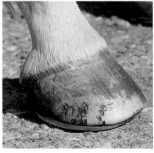

Note the way in which Natural Balance shoes are fitted.

of the sole and frog is no longer in contact with the ground, putting all the pressure on the hoof wall). It also identifies that these structures play a major role in supporting and protecting the fragile pedal bone.

The Natural Balance trim and shoes are designed to allow the horse to use these important supporting areas of his foot, rather than just relying on the hoof wall. The shoes are wide, particularly at the front, where they are set back from the toe to give maximum support to the pedal bone.

Heels and toes

Traditional shoeing tends to make the foot grow forward and lifts the frog off the ground. One of the aims of Natural Balance shoeing is to try to get the horse to land heel first and use his frog. Many horses do not do this and lack of use causes the frog to shrink, which is detrimental because the frog plays a vital part in the health of the foot. Its purpose is to suck blood into the foot, then push this blood to the front of the foot through the circumflex vessels and back up the vein. To make all these blood vessels work there must be pressure on the back of the foot.

The positioning of the front of a Natural Balance shoe is calculated to coincide with the horse's natural breakover point. This is the point just behind the toe where the foot pivots with the ground as it is lifted. Moving the shoe back and giving it a rounded edge is a reflection of the characteristic seen in wild horses' feet where the toe of the hoof wall is always worn away. Gene believes natural wear occurs in areas where excess growth would interfere with the horse's movement. By analysing limbs in motion he identified that long-toed horses found it more difficult to lift their feet off the ground. However, it should be borne in mind that his results are based on a single study that has not been duplicated. Further research is therefore needed to support these claims.

Cytek shoeing

The result of numerous worldwide studies of feral and semi-feral herds, the philosophy behind Cytek is simple (and very similar to Natural Balance): to create a shoe that allows the horse's foot to function as nature intended, supports the pedal bone and affords natural hoof growth, foot function, balance and movement.

Standardized shoes

The Cytek system is based on the belief that every horse and pony's foot is physiologically standardized (the position of the pedal bone, navicular bone, deep flexor tendon and so on), and so every Cytek shoe, of every size, is a standardized shape in order to support the bony column of the foot.

Cytek shoes are fitted precisely, without adjustment, and this is a key point. Rather than the shoe being shaped to fit an already deformed hoof, all Cytek shoes operate in the same way, whatever the horse's conformation or the shape of the hoof capsule. That is, they all support the pedal bone and are positioned well back, allowing the horse freedom to follow his natural point of breakover (something conventional rim shoes prevent) and wear down his feet at the toe as he would in the wild.

By enabling the horse's foot to function in much the same way as it would naturally, Cytek claims that many hoof problems associated with traditional shoeing such as collapsed heels, long toes, thin soles and stunted frog growth are eradicated. As a result of improved blood flow and hoof shape, hoof-related ailments such as corns, seedy toe, thrush, ringbone and even navicular disease are claimed to be eliminated with Cytek shoeing. On a broader note, Cytek claims that its shoes allow the horse to achieve his own central point of balance, in all paces and at all times, allowing him to carry himself in the best possible way. This reduces the risks of stresses and strains and has a beneficial overall effect on the horse's muscular and skeletal system.

The contrast between Cytek and conventional hind shoes is striking (left). All Cytek shoes are fitted in the same position: that's with one-third forward from the true base of the frog (where Cytek believes the centre of the foot to be – as shown by the dotted line above), and two-thirds back. This position allows the horse to wear his hoof at the toe as nature intended.

Cytek shoes support the bony column of the foot and allow the horse to follow his natural point of breakover (below).

Glossary

Understanding what is wrong with your horse can be difficult at the best of times, but it is even harder if the vet uses technical language that might as well be a foreign tongue to you. This guide will help you get to know your 'anterior' from your 'posterior'.

Abduct/adduct Describes the movement of a limb either away from the body (abduct) or towards the body (adduct). Your vet may use these terms when assessing lameness.

Acute Describes something being sharp in either its intensity or its severity. Generally used in reference to a sudden onset of disease or other problem.

Adhesion Bands of fibrous tissue in the body formed as a result of previous inflammation. These can join two structures together that should not normally be connected, resulting in a restriction of movement, or pain.

Analgesic Type of drug that is used to reduce or eliminate pain.

Anterior Describes the forward position of something, and is often useful in explaining the position of a structure in relation to other structures around it. Opposite to posterior (back/behind).

Arthritis Inflammation of a joint or joints, causing stiffness and pain. Equine arthritis is a broad term covering a range of joint disorders in the horse.

Aseptic Free from micro-organisms and bacteria that might otherwise contaminate, for example, a wound.

Ataxia Lack of muscle co-ordination, often due to disease or injury to the nervous system, which means the horse cannot move in an ordered way.

Atrophy Wasting shrinkage in the size of cells, tissues or a body part following paralysis of a nerve, when the muscles supplied by it cannot contract.

Bilateral Occurring on both sides. Can be used to describe a joint disease that is most likely to affect opposite limbs.

Biopsy Simple surgical procedure to remove a small section of tissue, so that it can then be analysed in a laboratory.

Bursa Sac containing fluid, usually found over bony prominences, which facilitates movement of tendons or muscles over bone.

Bursitis Inflammation of a bursa (see above).

Calcification Deposits of calcium in soft tissues or the deposition of calcium into swelling around joints, turning them into bone. Can be the result of certain types of osteoarthritis.

Cardiogram Graph that traces the activity of the heart as it is recorded using an instrument called a cardiograph.

Chronic Describes any disease or condition that is long term.

Collateral Running side-by-side (parallel); connected but secondary to a main course. For example, the pastern and coffin joints have two major ligaments, one on each side of the joint seen from the front, that are called the collateral ligaments.

Congenital Disease or defect that has existed since the horse's birth.

Congestion Abnormal accumulation of blood or fluid in a part of the body. A decongestant is a drug that relieves congestion.

Cyst Hollow sac containing fluid, semi-solid matter or air.

Degenerative joint disease (DJD) Form of osteoarthritis that is progressive and degenerative.

Distal Position of an injury or body part that is furthest away from an anatomical reference, for example 'the injury is distal to the hock'. The opposite is proximal, meaning nearest to.

Dorsal Relating to the back, or the front surface of the limbs.

Dysphagia Difficulty in swallowing.

Embolism Obstruction of an artery by a blood clot or other foreign matter.

Endocrine Any gland that secretes hormones into the circulation.

Enzyme Complex protein that acts as a catalyst to facilitate a specific action within body chemistry.

Exostosis Outgrowth of bone, such as a splint.

Fibrillation Rapid unregulated control of the heart chambers.

Fissure Crack or tear.

Fistula Channel that should not exist, but which communicates between two organs or an organ and the skin surface, as in a dental abscess.

Fluoroscopy X-rays strike a fluorescent plate that is coupled to an image intensifier and a TV camera. This allows instant viewing of the area and 'live' X-ray images, instead of a plain radiograph.

Gamma camera Detects the presence of gamma rays following injection of a radioactive substance. Used to locate areas of increased tissue activity (injury or disease), since 'hot spots' appear if there is an increased uptake of the radioactive compound.

Gastric Relating to the stomach.

Granulation Formation of too much tissue, produced as an injury repairs itself. The flesh can look granular and is also known as proud flesh.

Hyperextension Where a limb or joint has been extended beyond the natural range of motion. Similarly, hyperflexion is where a limb or joint has been overflexed.

Inflammation Reaction of living tissue to injury or infection, characterized by heat, swelling, redness and pain.

Intravenous Usually describes an injection directly into a vein.

Joint mouse Material (usually cartilage or bone) found in a joint space, which should not normally be present.

Laceration Wound formed by a tear to the skin.

Laser therapy Treatment of a body part using low-level (cold) laser, which emits light of a specific radio frequency.

Lateral Anatomical description of the position of a structure, meaning to the side.

Lesion Originally an injury but now applied to all changes produced by diseases in organs or tissues.

Magnetic Resonance Imaging (MRI) Diagnostic viewing technique that uses the effect of a supermagnet on the tissues of the body. Particularly good for visualizing soft tissue structures.

Metabolism Process of breakdown and synthesis within body cells that generates energy the body can use.

Necrosis Death of tissue within an area.

Neuralgia Pain along the course of a nerve.

Nodule Small swelling.

Nuclear scintigraphy Diagnostic technique for scanning bone, using a gamma camera (see above).

Osteoarthritis Full name for arthritis, in which the cartilages of a joint and adjacent bone are worn away.

Palpate To examine by touch, using the flat of the hand and fingers.

Pathogen Agent that causes disease.

Posterior see Anterior

Prognosis Prediction of the likely course of a disease and the chances of recovery.

Proximal see Distal

Purulent Full of, or discharging, pus.

Pyrexia Raised temperature or fever.

Radiography Producing an image on photographic film using an X-ray beam that passes through the part of the body to be examined.

Recumbent Lying down.

Rupture To burst, break or tear.

Spasm Involuntary muscle contraction.

Swab Sterile implement (like a large cotton bud) used to take a sample for analysis in a laboratory.

Systemic Relating to the entire body – a systemic disease or other problem would have repercussions throughout the body.

Thrombus Blood clot.

Tincture Alcoholic solution containing a drug.

Topical Generally used when describing the application of a drug (cream or similar) to the skin surface.

Trauma Wound or injury.

Ulcer Open sore on the skin or mucous membrane (for example, in the mouth).

Before...

If you see these common prefixes before a word, this is what they relate to:

Arterio- arteries
Arthr- joints
Chondro- cartilage
Derm- skin
Endo- inside
Epi- on top of
Gastr- stomach
Haem- blood
Hyper- increased
Hypo- decreased
Infra- below
Neuro- nervous system
Osteo- bones
Peri- adjacent to
Poly- multiple
Pyo- pus
Sub- below
Supra- above

and after...

This is what these common suffixes mean:

-itis inflammation
-oscopy visual examination
-ostomy making an opening into
-otomy incising into/through